SECOND PARENT

a memoir

LORA LIEGEL

For Finnley, my blazing sun.

Now you have my heart so full,
I'll love all the days from here and on,
Because a me gave way for three.

AUTHOR'S NOTE

When my wife and I began discussing how we would start a family, I looked for stories that were similar to my own experience – a lesbian, non-bio mom to-be. There were books for the gay and lesbian community on how to get pregnant or start a family. But I didn't find much specifically on the term "second parent," especially as it related to second parent adoption. Nor did I find much from gay parents written after same-sex marriage became legal in the U.S.

I began writing this book because I felt like the *other* mother. I wasn't just a mother to-be, I was a daughter trying to understand the relationship with the family I grew up with. I was trying to understand the meaning of the word *family*. I wondered if I could let go of old stories and write myself a new one.

After completing the second parent adoption process, I became even hungrier to read stories from my perspective. I could only find one other memoir in print, written by a lesbian non-bio mother, but it did not contain information specifically about second parent adoption. How could that be when becoming a parent is such a life-changing event?

What I hope is that we collectively question how legal and social landscapes view lesbian, non-bio mothers. Not being recognized as a parent can have serious ramifications for us and our children. We have unique histories but can be united by our common threads. For me, using the term *second parent* is about owning my role as a parent – seeing the value and worth that I possess.

I see courage in the act of sharing a voice. Pieces of our personal lives. There is power that comes from releasing a story. I share my truths in the hope that maybe, it will encourage someone else to share their own story too.

1

LET'S MAKE A BABY

My nerves were like a ball, banging around the inside of an old tin can. I felt restless. I felt tense. I sat in a chair pushed up alongside the flat, metal exam table and tried to focus my eyes on the beige wall a few feet ahead of me. The room lights were soft, intended to keep the patients calm. I appreciated that. But, I wasn't the patient.

My wife had her back on the table, her feet in the padded stirrups perched on top of metal rods shooting to the sky. Although Michelle probably should have been the one to be nervous, I was taking on that role like a champ. If everything went as planned, my wife would get pregnant. Today was the day we were going to make a baby, with a little help from science.

Today was *the day*. We had read about the odds and chances of Michelle getting pregnant. The fertility doctor said it could take six months or longer. That meant six or more expensive tries, one every month. Michelle had set the bar even lower, telling herself that it could take up to one year so she wouldn't be disappointed if it didn't take. But not me. This, our first attempt, would be the day our lives would change forever. Michelle was young and healthy. We were not typical candidates at a fertility clinic. We were two women in our early 30s. Plus, my wife had mentioned that women in her family were "extremely fertile." That sealed the deal. I was convinced that it was all happening inside that small exam room. I wouldn't officially know until two weeks later, when Michelle took a pregnancy test, but I was right. We would later joke about our *one-hit wonder*.

I was thankful that the nurse who walked in was smiling and made some lighthearted jokes. I felt nervous. I had done some reading on how the appointment might go, but it still felt like there were many unknowns. I didn't know if Michelle might experience pain. I didn't know if the medical staff was going to ask *me* any questions. I didn't know if we would see a doctor, or only a nurse. Mostly, I sat as a quiet observer, while my mind raced in several directions.

In that exam room, I was glad to be the non-biological parent to be. It felt like a role I could manage. A role I could handle. I felt a slight shudder when I thought about growing a baby inside my own body. The thought made me uncomfortable, because it made me think about my genes and what they might hold. At the clinic that day, I was not jealous that Michelle was on that table. But I was envious of how easily she had arrived at making the decision to be there.

I gave some comforting, reassuring pats to Michelle's arm and tried not to drip my sweaty mitts all over her. I whispered, "you're doing great" into the air, probably more to myself than to my wife. The nurse began to explain how she was going to do *the procedure*.

The procedure was an *intrauterine insemination*, commonly referred to as an "IUI." When I say commonly, I mean common to the type of people who happen to land themselves inside a fertility clinic. I hadn't heard of the term until we started doing some research a few months earlier.

The nurse's tone eventually became more professional. She looked at the charts and documents stuck to the clipboard. She asked us some questions. Inside her hand she held a clear vial. Although it was small, it contained millions of tiny sperm raring to go. Those sperm weren't average sperm. They had passed several medical tests, identifying them as strong candidates for doing the job. I liked to think of them as tiny Olympians sprinting for the finish line. Their prize: getting to nestle inside a giant egg, fertilization being their victory.

The sperm came from a reputable sperm bank. It had cost the equivalent of thousands of pennies dipped in medium-grade gold. Although the sperm bank provided the goods, they would not perform the actual insemination (baby-making part). That's how we ended up in a reproductive clinic located on the south end of Lake Union in Seattle, Washington.

At the time, my wife and I were living about ten miles east of the clinic. Michelle's ovulation cycle had ultimately dictated when we made the appointment, but I remember how we strategically chose a time that was in between work meetings and decreased our chances of sitting in traffic. How pragmatic we were! As we drove from East to West, I remembered being comforted by the lake's shoreline. We drove our bright blue Prius, identifying us as the good environmentally friendly, Northwest lesbians we were.

Our story of family planning was not much different than that of many other couples. We started dating, fell in love, got married, and began discussing the logistics of having kids. The primary difference was that we were two women. There would be no "accidental" pregnancies for us. There would be talking, planning, and research. Then more talking, more planning, and more research. Our logistics included how exactly we wanted to create our family. We discussed if either of us wanted to get pregnant, fostering, and adoption options too.

From the beginning, my thoughts about raising children had been more complicated than Michelle's. It had taken me longer to realize that children were indeed something I wanted in my life. As for bearing a child of my own, that gave me even greater pause. Did I ever want to get pregnant? I still hadn't decided. Michelle had always been open to giving birth to a child, and she was game. I was envious of Michelle's decision – how confident she was about it. With such little fear. But, it also made sense. Michelle was like that in every other aspect of her life. She was frequently cool, calm, and collected. We sometimes joked that she was like a robot, able to compute big and small decisions with ease. She didn't let insecurities or what ifs get in the way like I frequently did.

The primary reason I was hesitant about having children was that the foundation of my own childhood had some major cracks.

My mother lived with mental illness much of her life. Verbal and physical abuse had been rampant in my family growing up. A close look at my family tree also left me with questions.

My childhood weighed heavily on my mind, and I worried it would negatively affect my parenting abilities. It took me longer to want kids because I had to let the idea sink in. I told myself that if I committed to that path, I wanted it to be done right – it *had* to be done right. I wanted to give my kids everything that I didn't have growing up. I knew that raising a child was going to take financial, emotional, and physical responsibility. I wanted my kid to have stability. Ultimately, I wanted to provide a childhood better than my own.

For some, the desire for children is ever present, there from the beginning. But for others, including myself, that desire took longer to grow. Once it did, I felt it fiercely. It brewed inside me, as strong as a deliciously dark cup of coffee. At the age of 32, I had finally decided. I wanted to have a child, raise a family, be a parent, and be a mom. But I didn't want to get pregnant myself and this meant that I would never know my child in the same way as my wife. At least that's what I thought at the time. The one thing for certain was that I would never have a genetic connection to my kid. Out of all the decisions that I would make about becoming a parent, that felt like the one with the biggest implications.

We were not the first lesbian couple to start a family. So many queer women and men had paved the way to help us get there and yet sometimes it felt like the only family story I heard about, was one with a mother and a father living happily ever after. There was almost nothing to guide me on my journey of becoming a lesbian, non-biological mother-to-be. How was my experience going to be different from my pregnant wife? Would having no genetic connection to my child affect the way we interacted? Would it affect our future relationship? Would I always and forever be the "other" mother? The *second* parent?

2

BEGINNINGS

I grew up in a sleepy town, nestled among Willamette Valley farmland. Corvallis, Oregon. Situated just off a major highway and home to a university, the town was occasionally awakened by a baseball or football game, enough to fill the narrow streets and few hotels.

It rained most of the time. When the sun came out, everyone noticed. Swans landed in the green sprawling fields when they headed back north. My family and I would drive to see them each spring. I was amazed by their magnificent white wings and their ability to fly anywhere they dreamed.

On the east side of town there was a large Hewlett-Packard campus where many of my schoolmate's parents made their living. But not mine. My dad had a busy job with the government and my mom rarely worked outside our home.

SECOND PARENT

There were only two public high schools. One in town. And one on the north end, built among fields and forest. The town was small and quaint, characteristics that I did not appreciate until long after I had stopped living there.

While growing up, I wished I had more information about the missing pieces and branches of my family tree. When I was a kid, I gave little thought to who my parents were before I came into their lives. It's not that they didn't tell *any* stories about their pasts, it's that I couldn't put the revealed pieces into an integrated picture.

When I was about eight, I picked some gladiolas from our backyard. It was at the height of summer. The air touched my skin with a pleasant dryness as I ran my hands across the cool, pink petals. I felt joy and pride bringing them to my mother. I had picked them myself. But when my mother looked at the flowers in my hands, she said with sadness in her voice, "Those remind me of when my father died." Gladiolas had apparently been present at his funeral. The word *grief* was never discussed. As a child, I felt like I had made her sad. I loved flowers of every shape and size, but I walked away thinking, *Next year we shouldn't plant anymore gladiolas.*

I would later learn that my mother was just a child herself when her dad died by suicide. Only about twelve. After my grandfather's death, my mother, her two sisters, and her mother went to live with extended family. It was the 1950s in New York City and money was tight. There was not enough food to eat, and my grandmother had to find work. As the new head of household in an era when women rarely worked, I imagined the stress the entire family must have been under. But still, my mother rarely discussed her hardship. There were a few old, black and white photos from her past, but mostly it was just something she carried deep inside herself for all those years.

My father grew up in rural Ohio. He too had lost a parent when he was young, in his twenties. My father had escaped his parents who struggled with alcoholism by joining the seminary. As a young man in the priesthood, he didn't have to work on the family farm or be subjected to his father's verbal abuse. Like my mother, my father did not mention his upbringing much. My father's two brothers and my grandfather, still lived in Ohio, but he rarely mentioned them or his extended family. We visited a couple times when I was a kid, but I could tell he didn't share kinship or warmth with many of them.

When my dad was around, he did instill in me an appreciation of the natural world. We went to county parks, tulip fields, and iris gardens. We went berry picking in the summer. In fall, the two of us would find trees tucked away in alleys, heavy with fruit. I ate the bounty with delight. I enjoyed the feeling of finding something alive, which could slowly be savored. I understood that abundance should not be wasted.

My childhood mostly revolved around my mother's chaos. My mother struggled with bipolar disorder and compulsive hoarding. She received the bipolar diagnosis when I was four, but my parents never told me. I only later learned that detail when I was in my early thirties. My father escaped the chaotic situation by throwing himself into his work. He was frequently on business trips or traveling. I created a large scrapbook of all the postcards he sent me, but the foreign stamps and letters could never amount to enough. I needed him there physically and emotionally, and he wasn't.

In my teens, my father moved out of our house and into his own apartment at least three times. Instead of discussing the situation with me, my mother threw swear words into the air or threatened to slit her wrists. My father did not invite me over into his separate space, so I continued to endure the chaos of living with my mother on my own, after my sister moved out at the age of 16.

My sister Amy is almost six years older than me. In my early childhood years, the age gap felt big, and we were not close. After she moved out, I didn't see her much until I was about to start college.

My family life was not an example of what life should be. But I did see some glimpses from a different family. At the age of nine, I befriend a boy named Bobby at school. He and his parents welcomed me into their home with open arms. I spent many nights at their house eating family dinner or watching movies. They lived in the *nice* part of town, in a large house, and owned expensive things. They took me on their vacations to Yosemite, Yellowstone, and Tahoe. They went skiing in the winter. These were things that my family would never do. They showed me what life could be like with some stability. As a kid, I began to differentiate between normal and not normal. I identified that my home life was in the "not normal" category.

As an adult, that image of normal and not normal would stay with me. I knew that if I ever wanted to start a family, my primary goal, would be to embody normal. And as I got older, that definition took shape. I wanted to provide stability, love, and respect. I had spent *years* with shouting matches, hair pulling, and broken doors.

I carried a deep worry that if I had kids, I wouldn't have the skills to take care of them. I also worried that there was something hidden in my genes. A dark corner. A twisted branch. An unknown roll of the dice. If I had kids, would they have a propensity for depression? Would they have suicidal thoughts? Would they be emotionally or physically abusive? Would they turn out like my mother or other family members? If I had kids, would *I* turn out like my mother?

Before *Hoarders* was a hit TV show, I was living it out inside my childhood house. Unkempt stacks of newspapers littered the floor. Half-filled boxes reached the garage ceiling. Dust bunnies hopped across the linoleum. I had to walk on narrow paths through large stacks of debris to get to the kitchen or living room. As a child, I knew something was wrong, but I didn't know the condition had its very own name. As the years progressed, the house in which I lived from approximately age three to eighteen became less inhabitable. There was a pile of garbage outside our backyard window, covered by a cheap blue tarp that fluttered in the wind.

The director of operations in the house's growing mess was my mother. She didn't know how to throw anything away. An old dresser drawer. Receipts. Medicine bottles. Boxes. An expired can of beans. Files. Grocery bags. A holey coat. Wrappers, magazines, junk mail, tools.

The worst was newspapers. They faithfully arrived every morning, but never again left our house.

But an unkempt house was not the only issue. My mother struggled with time management and social norms. She was a compulsive shopper which meant that more than enough *stuff* always made it into our house. She had on again, off again, drinking problems.

In fifth grade, my 16 year old sister would pick me up from school in the family car, while my mother sat in the passenger seat. Amy would whisper in my ear, "Mom's been drinking again," then roll her eyes. At home, my mother would get an empty cup from the kitchen, then return from her bedroom with it full of liquid. Even though I hadn't heard the term "closet alcoholic," at the age of ten, I sensed that my mother was keeping secrets.

My mother was manic one day, depressed the next – sometimes violent, frequently unpredictable. She went through various dieting fads, but she was typically overweight. She dressed in men's slacks or oversized button-down shirts. She sometimes wore neon scrunchies in her hair. She liked to wear leather loafers. It was a casual, mismatched style which sometimes left me feeling embarrassed.

While she and Amy fought, her body seemed large and strong. Amy and I were the opposite, slender and petite. We were never a match for my mom's physical or emotional will.

Bipolar. Compulsive disorder. Mental illness. No one fits into only one box, and my mother was no exception. She continually lived with episodes of physical and mental illness. Her arms and legs were speckled with small, red sores. Sometimes they would break open and bleed, leaving red marks on her long sleeve shirt. She would scratch the sores on top of her head and I would sit in the backseat of the car, watching, and abhorred by her behavior. I did not understand the reasons for her physical ailments and no one in my family discussed them. It's possible that she was suffering from physical disorders, or the skin irritation could have simply been a condition related to the dusty and unkempt conditions we endured. Because it was so difficult to get actual information from my family, I will never know the true extent of my mother's illnesses.

When all else failed, my mother checked herself into the local hospital to get help. Fourth floor. Psych ward. From the little my mother told me; her own family had not fared much better. Her family tree was gnarled by homelessness, depression, addiction, incarceration, and suicide. But my mother rarely discussed her family members. The few family stories I had collected over the years, created a confused and disorienting puzzle.

Did my genetic family members make their choices because of a result of nature or nurture? If I had a biological baby, would it turn out like so many members of my family? With the few facts I had, I didn't think my genes were worth passing on.

When my mother wasn't going through a manic episode, she sometimes expressed kindness and compassion. We visited the downtown bridges and gave away food to the homeless. My mother possessed a unique sense of humor, so along with the canned goods, we also gave out the *National Enquirer Magazine*. She planted tomatoes in summer, and fed the birds in winter. She helped me develop my love for gardening and plants. My mother plainly taught me to see the value in food and people – even in the imperfect.

My mother volunteered with a local gleaning agency that helped deliver food to people with disabilities. She would cart me around to make drop offs when I had days off from school. We would visit a small community gathering place called The Iris Project, which gave out free meals to people who were homeless or living with mental illness. My mother never mentioned who the clients were, or why we were going. As the only kid there, I played pool or ate lunch with the adults. I sensed that the people were a little different, but because my mother and I never spoke about it, it wasn't noteworthy at the time. I just knew that if one person had extra food, it should be given to someone else who wanted it.

In my house, growing up, it wasn't just my mother who showed signs of distress. My sister too was often angry, depressed, and violent. The two of them fought incessantly. My mother would pull my sister's hair or push her to the ground. My sister would attempt to fight back, but it only further infuriated my mother. On one occasion, my sister picked up a steak knife and chased my mother into the master bedroom. I got caught up in their swirling vortex and became trapped in a tiny bathroom with my mother. The knife pierced the door and the memory haunted me long after. Although my mother was never directly violent toward me, I frequently became entwined with the two of them. I unconsciously attempted to protect my sister when I could, but as a younger sibling, I was much smaller and even less emotionally or mentally prepared to handle the situation than Amy was.

I never became accustomed to the flashing red and blue lights that bounced off the shadows of our cul-de-sac. The neighbors called the cops too many times to count. Flying words and fists left holes in our cheap, hollow doors. But I knew my place. I had carved it out myself.

I receded. I never shared my home life with anyone. I explored the natural world – hillsides, forests, farmland. I poured myself into school work and TV reruns. I wrote in my journals. I put my sights on moving out and entering college. I spent time with friends. Rode bikes. Joined sports teams. Played Frisbee and joined cross country. I learned to run.

Only later did I learn that self-preservation came at a cost. The cost being a need for rigidity and control. A constant questioning of choices made. An unwillingness to be vulnerable, because I didn't know what that word meant. My childhood was an old suitcase, dragging behind me. It didn't have wheels. It wasn't easy to pull. It was heavy and worn. It contained all my memories and stories from the past. No matter how hard I tried to shake it off, the handle loop wouldn't break free.

I first came out as gay when I was 23. Prior to that, I thought I was supposed to date boys. All my friends did. I wanted to experience what people around me were doing. I wanted to understand what *it* was all about. But *it* never felt right.

In college, a friend once confessed to me that she was having "boyfriend issues." She said, "we haven't slept together in a month," with a concerned look on her face. "Is that bad?" she asked. I felt like a deer in the headlights. Like she would see the deep lack of knowledge emanating from my pores. I was thinking, A *month? I haven't slept with anyone, ever.* Clearly, I was not an expert in these matters, but I tried to reassure her. "I'm sure it will be fine," I said. "You guys are great together."

When my best friend in college, Melissa, said she had *feelings* for me, I let the words sink in. They lingered longer than the time it took her to walk through my kitchen and close the door behind her. I had small moments where I had questioned my sexuality before, but I hadn't let my mind wander too far. I had laid in bed one evening, a little before Melissa was in my life and thought, *I wonder if I like women.* It was a fleeting thought. I was so disconnected from my emotions, the thought simply came and went.

The first time Melissa and I kissed, I felt electricity. I was sold. I was all in. We dove headfirst, into a three-year-long romantic relationship. But our years of friendship and shared experiences were not enough to sustain us. In that time, I lacked the awareness to see how my past was affecting my current relationship. The past was influencing my desire to control many aspects of my life. I always wanted to know what the *plan* was. It left little room for surprise and a big hole for fear to take its place. Melissa surmised that my childhood and relationships with my family members were rocky, but never asked questions. I figured that if I could keep my family at bay and out of our lives, then it wouldn't matter. But it did. Although my lack of self-awareness was one of the reasons Melissa and I broke up, it was not the only one. When Melissa quickly started dating a man after we parted ways, I was crestfallen. My insecurities were sparked. *Had she ever loved me?* I wondered. Only in time did I realize that love is allowed to come and go.

For so many years of my youth, I had taken care of myself. I cooked when there wasn't dinner on the table. I cleaned when the house became too messy. I drove myself to appointments if I wanted to show up on time. I'd let my relationship with Melissa take a substantial portion of my independence. I had fallen in love but given up my self-reliant spirit in the process. In short, we had become codependent. Melissa and I did most things together, like visiting the farmers market, taking a walk, or going to the grocery store. It left little time for either of us to establish meaningful relationships outside our own.

I realized I needed help. Help to move forward. Help to find myself again.

At the time, I was enrolled in graduate school in the heart of the redwood forests of northern California. Although my studies in a social science program sometimes took me to rural Idaho, the bulk of my work and classes were based in Arcata. On the first day of fall session, in my second year of grad school, I called the university counseling center and made an appointment.

With a therapist's help, I slowly started building the tools I needed to get back on my feet. I joined an LGBT club on campus. I came to the realization that I hadn't just lost a girlfriend, I was grieving the loss of our family unit. *Family.* Family had always been such a complicated word for me, and that loss hit me the hardest.

First, I did what I knew how to do best. I moved. I put my body in motion. I started cycling. I started running long distances. I'd lace up my shoes and hit the road. I would run six, seven, eight miles at a stretch. Starting at my house, I'd make my way to the farmland bottoms. The landscape wasn't burdened by houses or people. It felt clean. It felt inviting.

After being with Melissa, I dated a few other women. But, those relationships only lasted a few months. However, one of these short-lived relationships did leave a lasting impression on me.

While still in grad school, I briefly dated a woman named Sarah, with chestnut colored hair and an attractive, positive spirit. She was a few years older than me and was clear about wanting to start a family – and soon. This caused me to have fleeting thoughts about having children and what that might look like, including potential sperm donors in my life.

Initially, I thought that if I used donor sperm, I wanted to know the person donating, as opposed to using an anonymous donor. I liked the idea of strong connections between friends, nature, and community. I didn't think the donor would be a "dad," but more like a semi-involved uncle. I figured that if I ever had children of my own, whether they came from my body or not, they were going to be raised in a nontraditional household because they would have two moms. Maybe having a third adult figure could be a positive influence. I thought that having a relationship with the donor would be important to my hypothetical children.

Ultimately, it was Sarah's desire to have kids that prompted me to end the relationship. I decided I wasn't ready to have children yet. After finishing grad school, getting through a breakup, and surviving small town living, I was ready for a change. Ready to return to the true Northwest. Portland, Oregon, also known as, The City of Roses, had been calling my name for months.

I almost missed meeting my future wife. A friend challenged Michelle to go on four dates in a single month. I had messaged *threemadronas* on an online dating site, but she had ignored my first request. I thought that was odd because we were a 90 percent match! As the days of the month ticked by, and at the prospect of not meeting her quota, Michelle finally responded. But by that time, I was about to leave for a trip to Alaska. I suggested we go on a date when I return. I hoped she would still be free when I got back. Luckily, she was.

For our first date, I chose a bar close enough to my house, so I could bike. I had a constant fear I would be late. As a result, my propensity for showing up early left me plenty of time to spare.

I found a small table on the back patio, ordered a vodka soda, and busted out some reading material. Yep. I brought magazines to my date. I waited in nervous anticipation. I imagined Michelle strolling up. "Oh, nice to meet you," I'd say. "I'm just casually reading magazines in my spare time. At a bar." She would respond, "That's so cool!" I knew it was goofy, but I wanted to demonstrate the confidence I had worked hard to build. I wanted to show my independence.

The time ticked by. Just as I thought I was being stood up, Michelle came over and introduced herself. We exchanged some jokes and laughs. It felt easy. Later I discovered that Michelle thought she was being stood up too. She had been sitting up front at the bar, and texted to ask where I was. But I hadn't brought my phone. Luckily, she had the wherewithal to check the back. *Street smarts*. Check.

The woman before me was cool, confident, and charming. Her

smile had a hint of mischievousness. Her brown hair was cut short, but had that feminine flare I was looking for. She was cute. She wore a plain dark red t-shirt, and a few simple rings on her fingers. I liked her style. I could tell she had previously worn a lip ring, by the tiny scar it left behind. I was intrigued. I wanted to hear the stories coming from that mouth.

We played a round of ping-pong and exchanged serves and witty banter. I had found someone equally as competitive as me. A worthy opponent. Someone who was willing to challenge me, but do it with a smile on her face, and leave me wearing one too.

After two drinks, I said I had to leave. I figured the date was going so well, I didn't want to ruin it. I told this to Michelle, who thought this concept was flawed. I could later see her logic, but didn't at the time. We walked out of the bar together and headed toward the bike rack. She had biked too! We both put on our helmets. *Safety first!* Check. The stars had aligned. It was a solid beginning.

On our second date, we met at a small Thai food restaurant. I wasn't going to order a drink because I wanted to see how our connection was without the influence of alcohol. When the waiter came by to take our order, Michelle said she just wanted water. I thought, *Score! This girl is on my page!* A few weeks later, Michelle told me she hadn't ordered a drink because she was getting over giardia. I thought we had both wanted clear minds, but it was Michelle's overconfidence in drinking unpurified water while backpacking, that had ultimately been behind the decision.

At the end of the same date, we headed for our parked bikes.

Before Michelle hopped on, I leaned in and gave her a kiss. She literally stumbled. I thought, *Damn! I'm good!* Turned out, Michelle was just plain clumsy.

Date number three was dinner at my house, date number four was watching leaves fall at our neighborhood park. I stopped counting dates, and by month six, we had Defined the Relationship (DTR'd). I deleted my online dating account where we had first "met." There were mix-ups and misunderstandings, but we kept coming back to one another.

Eventually, the conversations turned toward family and what our future might hold. My childhood past. My apprehensions. I had spent years avoiding the emotionally painful stuff with friends and previous people I had dated. Michelle was the first person I shared my childhood stories with.

Michelle and I had been dating about a year, when we went camping together outside of Bend, Oregon. It was summertime and the high desert air was dry. We found a half-empty campground and popped our tent amidst the ponderosa pines. Michelle pronounced that she wanted to have kids. It wasn't a proclamation or big announcement, it was simply a fact. The moment stuck, because it was the start of a longer-term conversation, one that we would revisit as our two paths intertwined. The generality that had surrounded those questions started to disappear. They took on specificity. I asked myself, *Do I want to raise children and start a family with this woman lying beside me? Do I want to be a biological mother?*

By my late twenties, many of my friends who were a few years older than me began having kids of their own. The more I was around their babies, the more comfortable I became around kids. Up until then, the idea of holding a baby was terrifying. What exactly was I supposed to do with *it*? What if it started crying? What if I dropped it?!

I liked rules. I liked knowing what was coming next. I had a feeling that if I became a mother, I was going to have to give up some of that knowing.

As I lay in the tent on that summer afternoon, I sensed that the hidden grandness of the discussion about children could make or break our relationship. If we decided to travel on the path to parenthood, it would take a good amount of planning. I would have to give up some of my control. Michelle would have to give up some of her fierce independence.

3

HOME

What makes a house, a *home*? A house is filled with stuff. A TV, tables, some chairs, a kitchen sink, old newspapers. A home is where you share memories. It's full of life. Full of energy.

For years, as an adult, I tried to protect the spaces I lived. It didn't matter the city or state. Where I lived was more than a house with four walls. It was my safe space. It was where I felt protected from the world. It was an area that I could control. It was mine. My mother nor my family members were living inside it with me. And this felt the most important. I was free from their oppression, anger, and abuse.

Even when I lived with housemates, I always had my own room. After spending my childhood under a roof that was cluttered and dysfunctional, living on my own meant I could clean up any mess, to my full heart's content. Everything always had an organizational system. I knew where items were supposed to go – which shelf the coffee grinder should sit on. That the soap dispenser should be on the left side of the sink. That garbage cans went out on Tuesday night. I felt the power in making a million tiny decisions. My feelings of fearing the unknown, which began when I was a kid, still remained. They had served me well as a child trying to survive the dysfunction, but it was hard to let them go as an adult.

There is nothing like an organizational spree to fill me with a sense of order. I love checking tasks off a list. When all my tasks are complete, I feel accomplished. But when things cannot be completed in a day, or checked off the list, the uneasiness sets in.

Over a span of 15 years, I had lived in over 20 places. Some spots were more memorable than others. But each home had its own nickname or point of reference. There was The Hacienda, Bamboo Palace, Easy Street, Yosemite, Highland, Ashton, Brooklyn, and Albina.

But there had been previous houses. Ones that didn't feel as safe. Spaces I had to work harder to protect. There was a time when I lived on my own, but still in the same town as my mother. She would swing by to drop things off on my front porch. A gift can be nice. But the items were random and cheap – at least to me. To my mother, each item had been hand-picked at the store, because it reminded her of me. A pack of hand towels with seashells on them. A wind-up toy. A can of beans. A pack of gum. A live tree. A winter coat, size XXL (I wear medium). My mother didn't respect boundaries – emotional, physical, or mental. I always carried fear that when she stopped by to drop off a bag stuff, she would cause

26

a scene. That she would ask weird questions which would make me feel embarrassed. When my roommate commented on the alarming number of odd items on our doorstep, I would quickly try to laugh it off. I'd think, *Next subject, please.*

From my mom, I would hear: "Oh it's just a little something. Take it."

"Taking it won't *kill* you."

"You need this!"

I would repeatedly tell her that I appreciated the sentiment, but I didn't want the stuff. I tip-toed around her, without setting clear boundaries myself. I was afraid of what might happen if she felt upset. She would say, "Okay, okay," then not deliver anything for a couple weeks. But then she would go shopping again, and the cycle would repeat. It was a constant battle. A constant frustration. It wasn't just about wanting to be on my own like a lot of young adults. It was about protecting myself – my privacy and my space too. I occasionally tried to explain the concept of boundaries, but it never worked. She didn't get it. She always had a way of justifying her actions.

When I moved to remote Northern California, I felt a new-found freedom. The ruggedness of the landscape dotted with redwoods and ocean beaches made the location difficult to access. I could close my door, lock it, and not worry about my mother stopping in. She only *popped by*, unannounced, once.

I could be anyone. Do anything. But I was also hiding my family from friends and other important people in my life. With the aid of the therapist, I realized there were stories that needed to be told. I didn't have to keep them secret anymore. I could share my past with those I trusted, without fear of judgement. In the right moments, I could be open and honest. When I revealed my truths, other people told me theirs. I learned that many of my friends also had family members who lived with mental illness.

The relationship I developed with Michelle was forged from a solid foundation. Instead of hiding details and skirting difficult conversations, I began to tell the truth. I had met someone who was willing to hear my stories and be a supportive partner. Part of it was her. But a big part of it was me. I was finally ready to start building something new. Letting go of the past, opened up space. It left room for me to write new definitions of *Family. Parent. Mother.*

The first time Michelle came over, she noticed that I kept my socks in a bucket. Not a nice-looking bucket with a wicker trim. But a bright orange plastic one from Home Depot that probably cost me two dollars. Buying a dresser was a waste of money and an unnecessary possession. My youthful self was a cheap minimalist. Michelle and I were similar. So much so, a few months later, she confessed to having kept her socks in a bucket too! Michelle secretly wondered if she was dating someone too similar to herself. The thought had crossed my mind too.

People told us that we looked similar. I have a slightly more slender build and longer hair. But we are virtually the same height and weight. Our faces both show our German heritage. Her Finnish ancestry mixes things up, but I hated being asked if we were related.

"No, she's not my sister. She's my girlfriend!" I would say to those that asked. The first time Michelle introduced me to her parents, I overheard her mother say to a friend, "They're like twins!" I rolled my eyes and hoped she didn't see me. I knew we were similar, but I wanted to be recognized for me. Just because we were two women who were dating, didn't mean we were indistinguishable.

Mostly, I wondered if we were too similar in our desires or expression. For example, I typically liked things *my way*. Although Michelle was more go with the flow, she was a natural leader. She was the one who organized backpacking trips for her friends or invited people over for a dinner night. If we were going to be in a committed relationship, each of us would have to take turns leading and following.

With time, we carved out time to learn from one another, in between the space of familiarity. But it wasn't always easy. I still enjoyed planning dates and figuring out what might come next. But little by little, I learned that unexpected moments could lead to adventures. Although Michelle enjoyed aspects of planning, she was much more open to spontaneity. I learned from her that the unknown can leave room for playfulness and joy. But it was our similar life-views and values that kept me coming back for more.

Michelle had a huge heart for animal welfare and human rights. The thought of cows in cages or hungry children made her cry. Michelle was funny and kind. She was logical to a point of annoyance, but damn it if she wasn't always right. She made the best vegan muffins. She knew how to make balloon animals. She had once been a sailing instructor. She was the least stressed person I knew. I fell in love with her sense of calm, as it balanced my over-anxious spirit. She was also the most fiscally responsible twentysomething I knew and encouraged me to open a retirement savings account. *Who does that?*

When Michelle and I met, she worked for a recycling and composting company. She knew all the best spots for free dumpster food. This knowledge was originally spurred by a lack of income while previously working for AmeriCorps. But she also genuinely disliked unnecessary waste. Our love for food was something we shared.

For almost the entirety of my career I had worked in the agricultural sector. I had an incredible appreciation for how humans grow food and the resources it takes. At the time, I was working for a berry crop consulting company in Portland. While scoping out plants for pests and diseases, I regularly picked a few extra berries to bring back for Michelle. Michelle's appreciation for food, especially the end products like compost, was a perfect pairing for my own love of food and farming.

With time, Michelle and I built trust. One of my favorite dates with her included dumpster diving. I learned that she would be there to catch me, even if it was to jump into a two-foot pile of day-old bagels. She was frugal and thrifty to an extreme. She regularly ate "Dumpster Pizza." While pedaling home from the bars, she would shout to me and our friends, "Who wants DP?!"

I thought I had a busy social life, but she was out with friends every night of the week. I liked that she was independent, but I wondered if there would be enough room for our relationship to grow. For it to turn into something serious.

As the months went by, I started to imagine what a family with her might look like. I started answering the questions that arose from that initial camping trip. If we had a family, the kids would be well taken care of. Michelle would love them with compassion and kindness. I imagined us working as a team. Michelle had all the qualities that would make her good parent material.

But I also wondered what I would contribute. *What would be my role? What were the skills I had?* Michelle's most valuable quality (that I would later envy), was her ability to be patient, even in the most difficult situations. As for me, I liked to think of myself as calm on the outside, but humming and buzzing on the inside. I sometimes felt bursts of anger but instead of letting it out, I'd bury it under my skin. This caused conflict in our relationship, but we had always been able to work through it.

When Michelle and I had been dating two years, I told her that I wanted to live together. I felt that I couldn't know that I wanted kids with Michelle, before we lived under the same roof. Michelle didn't want to live together under that roof before she knew I wanted kids. We were in a bit of jam. Something had to give. Everything came to a head when Michelle decided to buy a house.

Michelle, being the fiscally responsible gem she is, decided it was time to diversify her assets. She went on a home-purchasing quest, and I wondered how I would fit into that quest. If Michelle wasn't ready to live together after buying a house, I knew it was time for me to say goodbye.

One night I finally told her where I stood – what was at stake. We shared an intimate conversation and both concluded we weren't ready to end the relationship.

Michelle purchased a house that spring, and we moved in together. The 1920s home desperately needed work. We tore up carpet. Sanded floors. Painted windows. Ripped up weeds. In a single month, with the help of Michelle's family and our friends, we turned that house into a home. Michelle had a strong work ethic. She was committed. When she saw the potential in something, she could turn it into a beautiful, functioning reality. In a way, that house was our relationship. We worked on it. We fixed it up.

After a few months, Michelle exclaimed that living together wasn't so bad after all, and we should have moved in together sooner. I thought, *yeah obviously, that's what I have been saying!* But I phrased my actual excitement differently.

Michelle's hesitations were disappearing. And so were mine. After living together, I started to see our future even more. But if we were going to have kids, I wanted to get married. I didn't know exactly what our future family would look like, but I increasingly suspected that I wouldn't be the birth-mom.

4

WORTH THE WAIT

After living together for a few months, our conversations about marriage and kids became more frequent. Michelle was comfortable with the idea of having kids without being married. But, initially, I was not.

Michelle was resistant to the idea of marriage because she had reservations about the concept of "forever." At first when I heard this, it made me question how much she valued our relationship. It made me question how much she valued *me*. "What do you mean we're not going to be together forever?" I asked. If she felt that way, how could I trust her, or have faith in our relationship? But as I sat with her hesitation, I began to understand what she really meant.

In today's modern era, it is increasingly easier for a woman to live her own life. She doesn't have to have a man or a woman by her side. She can have her own job, house, friends, community, and even a baby. The more we talked about commitment, the more we were able to articulate what that word meant to each of us. With time, we got on the same page.

Commitment, we decided, meant acknowledging that there would be tough times and good times too. It wasn't only saying yes to the big moments in life (saying I love you for the first time, getting married, or even having a child), but saying yes to all the smaller moments in between the big ones. Commitment was about appreciating the present, valuing the future, and recognizing our limits. If we were together for ten or twenty years, but were miserable in our daily lives, we would separate, doing whatever was best for us and our children. Instead of feeling guilty, or like societal failures, why not celebrate that the relationship had lasted as long as it did?

Just as I was getting ready to accept the idea that Michelle and I would have kids, but would not get married, she proposed. Michelle had recently accepted a job near Seattle and we would move there together in less than two months. Living together had brought us closer than we ever had been. The house had come a long way and so had our relationship too.

We were finishing up a painting project when Michelle asked if I wanted to go on a picnic. After a hot shower, I decided I was too tired to leave the house. But Michelle persisted and I gave in.

We walked to our neighborhood park and sat on a bench under tall trees. The last of the fall roses were blooming. The yellow leaves had just started falling. This was the same park where we had spent a memorable fourth date, basking in the sun and newness of our relationship.

Michelle pulled out a few snacks from her backpack, then fell silent. I knew something was up as she turned away from me to dig in the backpack some more.

"Why are you being so quiet?" I asked with a grin on my face.

"Just give me a minute," she said, while smiling. Maybe I imagined it, but her hands looked like they were slightly shaking. She turned back toward me and pulled two silver rings from her pocket. As they lay in her palm, she asked simply, "Do you want a ring?"

"Yes, I do," I said, and slipped on the silver band. The rings and moment fit us both.

In a few short weeks, Michelle and I organized a small gathering of family and friends to watch us get married, but mostly it was an excuse to eat a delicious dinner at one of our favorite neighborhood restaurants.

I felt confused about whether to invite any of my family members. I didn't want to feel anxious, worried, or embarrassed on the day I got married. My mother and father had not seen each other in at least ten years. By then, my father had entered into a serious relationship and my mother had rekindled a spark with a long-time friend and had since gotten remarried. However, my mother's husband was falling ill to Parkinson's and was mostly bed ridden. Although my mother had a difficult enough time caring for herself, she had assumed responsibility of her husband's care too. She occasionally hired part-time help, but had only left him overnight one time.

Ultimately, I decided to invite my father and sister, but not my mother. I told my mother that the event would be small. I understood it would be difficult for her to find more help. We could celebrate together another time, in our own way. Although I said all these things, the truth was, I didn't want my dad, sister, mother, and myself in a single room together. It felt like too much of a risk to my emotional and mental well-being. I feared there would be yelling, awkward stares, or possibly an uproar. I pushed through the guilt of not inviting my own mother to my marriage day and tried to move forward.

Before we headed to the park to get married, Michelle ate a giant bowl of borscht soup. Out of all the things she could have eaten, she chose bright red root vegetables. I asked her why she had chosen it and she said, "There were leftovers in the fridge." Even on a day most people feel nervous or overwhelmed, she continued to be practical and relaxed. I asked her to please wipe her face so we could get going. I was feeling anxious about showing up on time.

It was the end of November 2015, when we returned to the park where we had gotten engaged. With Michelle's family in tow, we walked from our house to the park. The sun shined and the air was crisp and clear. The remaining guests met us there wearing silly hats, which we had requested. Michelle and I each wore casual clothes and trucker hats that said, *BRIDE*. Our officiant showed up wearing a two-foot-wide rainbow head piece. We exchanged our vows. The ceremony was done in less than ten minutes. Our guests clapped, a friend handed us each a cup of cheap champagne. Our wedding was short. It was organized with little planning. But somehow, it felt perfect.

And so, with every intention that we would stay together, grow old together, and laugh together, we married. One week later, I made a joke about how it had taken three years for Michelle to bring the U-Haul. It was worth the wait.

With silver rings and boxes packed, we headed to Washington. Shortly thereafter, we got down to the nitty-gritty of how we wanted to create a family. We discussed all the options.

After a few months of temporarily staying with Michelle's aunt, we moved to a lakeside neighborhood in Kirkland, a few miles east of Seattle. We rented one of the few remaining small ranch homes. The rest had been bulldozed, making space for newly built mansions. We knew we wouldn't be able to stay forever, being at our rental budget's max. But I savored the lake view and space for a garden, not believing our luck in having found such a spot. That small house on the hill, became our family's first home.

5

LOGISTICS

When I don't know something, I tend to feel lost. I want stories, facts, figures, and maybe even a little humor to get me oriented. No two stories are ever alike, but surely there were lesbian couples before us who had gone through this. But when I looked for those stories outside our small circle, particularly in print, there were surprisingly few.

A few months before we left for Seattle, I started doing some research. I looked on Google and Amazon. I went to the library. I reached out to lesbians who had already had children. Michelle stumbled onto a book geared toward lesbians trying to get pregnant. By this time, the book was already ten years old, but we found some of the stories helpful. It dug into the specifics: the pros and cons of choosing an anonymous donor versus someone you knew, where prospective parents can purchase sperm and how much it costs, what types of insemination, and associated medical interventions there are. Instead of stating what *should* be done, the author laid out several scenarios about what *could* be done for each.

Educating myself about the details of what getting pregnant might be like for one of us, helped reduce some of my fear about the process.

During that same summer, I had quit my job at the crop consulting company to work at an urban farm in northeast Portland. I listened to the audiobook while picking tomatoes in the hot sun. Michelle listened to the book while sanding and caulking windows of her new house. In the evenings, we would swap stories about what each of us had read (or listened to) – what we thought and what we liked. We described what connected for us. Life was ridiculously busy, but we were learning. We were turning an idea into action.

Eventually, my thoughts on what I wanted my family to look like evolved. Part of this was because I was no longer single, or as independent as I used to be. I was in a committed relationship with two people's opinions to consider. The what ifs were becoming realities. I needed to make actual decisions that would affect not only myself, but also Michelle and our future children.

I recognized that people's lives change. The longer you live, the more complex your life gets. We have all had friends that we felt extremely connected to, but then one day you realized that they were hardly in your life at all. You used to talk every day. Then it was once per week. Then once per month. By the time the new year was being rung in, you couldn't even remember the last phone call, email, or text. Friends get involved with activities, partners, and work. Could Michelle and I count on a known donor sticking around for our kid? Could they honor a life-long agreement? If friendship fallouts could happen, it seemed likely that it could happen with a known donor too.

Despite the potential challenges, donor arrangements do exist. I knew one lesbian couple whose brother donated sperm to his sister's female partner. When I first heard about this arrangement, I thought it was a little strange. But after examining my own judgment about what a family should look like, I got past this opinion. The couple had tried to conceive using a different donor for quite some time without success. They let go of their first idea and decided to try something different. When I thought about it more, it was novel. The kids would end up sharing genetic qualities from both their mothers, a rarity among same-sex partners. I also assumed that because the donor was one of the women's brother, there would be fewer risks with the donor falling out of touch with their family.

Some of my friends had made more casual, verbal agreements with sperm donor acquaintances. One couple I knew asked an acquaintance whom they respected to use his sperm and he said yes. It took an eight hour drive to meet up, but in doing so, they received a fresh sperm donation which had resulted in the woman getting pregnant. No contracts were drawn. The man had wanted to help someone, but made it clear he didn't want to be in any future children's lives.

Over the years, Michelle and I had each accumulated stories about what worked and didn't work between lesbian mothers and their sperm donors. We needed to decide what kind of relationship seemed best for us. We had an idea about what we wanted, but still needed more information.

My wife and I discussed all potential algorithms for creating a family. We investigated adopting a baby, but the potential costs seemed higher than we could afford. At minimum, twenty or thirty thousand dollars, likely more. We discussed fostering, but Michelle increasingly expressed a desire to get pregnant. She took the lead on initiating child-making discussions. She was the one who started researching sperm banks.

At the time, I was still on the fence about my own womb-bearing capacity. I still needed time to think about whether I wanted to take a chance, by passing on my genes. We wanted to have a child sooner rather than later, so I continued to ponder my thoughts, while we moved forward with the process. The more we discussed our options, it seemed clear that we would need to find a sperm donor. From the webpages and books I read, I learned that a donor can play a significant role as a parent, have limited contact, or none.

I said goodbye to one idea in particular; using donated sperm from one of my male friends. He was tall, blonde, smart, and even had some familial ties to a famous musician. I thought, *could our future baby be a pop star?* Not that I really wanted that, but it was fun to think about. But after reading the book about how lesbians could get pregnant, we learned about what the logistics might be like if we tried to conceive with him.

For starters, we did not live in the same location. He would have had to send the sperm via mail using liquid nitrogen to temporarily freeze his little swimmers. In theory, that could have worked. However, we heard stories about sent sperm arriving with questionable quality – the sperm arriving dead, damaged, or with a low count.

An alternative to mailing sperm was flying to a common geographic location once per month, so he could give a more, *fresh* specimen. I would have wanted to be there to provide moral support, but if my partner didn't get pregnant in the first few months, those flights could have gotten expensive very quickly. It was also logistically difficult because most ovulating women only have a narrow window during the month (48 hours) when they are most fertile and ready to conceive. We didn't know if it would take Michelle a month to conceive, or a year, or even longer. Planning flights around a potential fertility window seemed questionable at best.

It was the idea of what a future connection between us, the donor, and our child might look like that led us away from using a known donor. If we used a known donor who was a friend, their would be many perspectives to keep track of. If friendships had faded over time, it seemed likely that a relationship with a known donor may also fade with time. I didn't want us to get into a situation where our child had regular meet ups with a known donor over the first few years of their life, only to be disappointed when the meet ups occurred less frequently or stopped all together. It seemed like that might be more confusing or emotionally difficult for a child, than if the relationship was more black and white from the beginning. Michelle and I found ourselves more interested in using an anonymous donor from a sperm bank.

To better understand her cycle, Michelle tracked her period using a simple smartphone app. This gave us an idea about which days she would ovulate each month. In addition, she used the "pee stick method." There were several brands of ovulation sticks that existed. We chose one that was recommended by a fertility specialist. It was simple. Pee on the stick and see an empty circle, or pee on the stick and see a happy face. A happy face meant that the woman's *LH surge* was occurring. We hadn't heard of the LH surge before, but learned that it stands for Luteinizing hormone. In layman terms, the LH surge is what gets ovulation going. This surge happens right before the egg drops, which is an ideal time to get inseminated or have sex. The timing was ideal for sperm and egg to meet, increasing chances of fertilization. Using the period tracking and pee stick method made me feel like we were *in charge* of the pregnancy process. Of course, these were only tools which could help Michelle conceive, not guarantees of that outcome.

By the time Michelle was peeing on sticks, we decided for sure that we wanted to use an anonymous donor. We decided with certainty that it was too big of an ask for any of our friends, near or far. We also wanted sole custody and parental rights to our child. This would have meant having the man sign away his. Our friendship would have been altered forever, and we just weren't willing to gamble that. Choosing an anonymous donor seemed legally cleaner and logistically easier.

Once we decided we wanted to use an anonymous donor, we had to choose where to purchase the sperm. There were several sperm banks throughout the United States. Most were for-profit companies and some were non-profits (these tended to charge less).

There were several factors that were important to us in choosing a bank. Above all geographic location, the number of available donors, and the frequency at which the donors provided samples.

At the time, I'd learned about a sperm bank that seemed like a good fit. They had a great website: it was modern, convenient, professional, and easy to use.

The sperm bank had a fair number of donors to choose from. For about $50, we signed up for a three-month online subscription that allowed us to view donor profiles, which included genetic background, handwritten responses to sperm bank questions, audio files of the donor voice, and baby photos of the donor. It reminded me of an online dating profile.

The sperm bank also included details about donor ethnicity, education, profession, height, weight, and hair color. The sperm bank provided information on how many vials of sperm were available and if the donor's sperm had resulted in a previous pregnancy.

The website also explained with detail the distinct types of insemination and their associated costs. There were two primary approaches that the sperm bank offered: intrauterine insemination (IUI) and intracervical insemination (ICI).

With ICI, the sperm is injected into the cervix, which can be done at home or at a medical clinic. With IUI, the sperm is injected directly into the uterus by a nurse or physician. Although IUI is more expensive, it's believed that this procedure has a slightly higher success rate than ICI. In addition, IUI and ICI samples were either "washed" or "unwashed." Washing removes slow or dead sperm and other content such as white blood cells that may interfere with the fertilization process. Each step that increased our chances of getting pregnant cost more money. We weighed the financial and emotional costs of each option.

The other factor in deciding to use the sperm bank was that the process was not totally anonymous. When our child turned 18, he or she could request information about the donor from the sperm bank. Per contract, the donor had agreed to meet any of the resulting children at least once.

I believe that most people have an inherent desire to know where they come from – to know their history, even if it's truncated. This includes knowing about background, familial history, and biological makeup. Although these things don't determine someone's future, they are intriguing.

I imagined that our child would have questions about why he or she has two moms, or alternatively why he or she does not have a dad. I didn't know how my child would think about the donor, but felt open to having conversations about him. I imagined that I would tell my child that many children only live with their mom, and some live with their grandparents, and some are adopted, and some only live with their dad. I imagined that my child would be filled with questions. Getting to meet the donor once, could maybe answer a few of them.

As an adult, I recognized there were questions I would probably never get answers to. Why was my own mother so unstable? Why did my grandfather take his life? What are my aunts and cousins really like? On my path to parenthood, I began to accept what I did not know. However, in my teens and twenties, it was different.

I always wanted more – more answers and more information. I guessed that my future child would feel similar. If my child could meet the donor once, maybe there would be a possibility of comfort or resolve of unanswered questions.

6

THE PLAN

After we had gotten married and moved to Washington, Michelle wanted to get pregnant as soon as possible. I was excited, but also felt some apprehension. Choosing a donor meant that we were getting that much closer to having an actual baby. The idea that our lives would drastically change, started to sink in. I didn't want to back out or not have a family, but I did start feeling some fear about how our relationship would change. I assumed there would be less time for us as a couple. There would be less free time in general. But, the rewards of being a parent still outweighed the option of not creating a family with children.

Buying the sperm and getting inseminated was going to be expensive. That's why we were willing to spend more money at the beginning of the process if it meant increasing our chances of getting Michelle pregnant sooner. If Michelle didn't get pregnant after several months of trying, we would reevaluate our plan (such as trying at home instead of using the medical clinic).

We decided to use a donor who had several IUI samples available in case the first few inseminations didn't result in pregnancy. In the end, we bought three IUI samples which were from a single donor. We also found out that this donor had more sperm in quarantine, which would be available in the future.

I learned that sperm banks can have different waiting list rules. For example, a donor's sperm might not be available for the public to purchase. However, if you already have a child using a donor's sperm, you may be able to get on the waiting list for more.

When Michelle got home from work each night, we would use our three-month all access pass. By this time, it was deep fall. It was dark and rainy. We would curl up by the fireplace, laptop in hand, imagining what our future child could be like. Choosing a donor was a big decision, but it didn't feel like work. There were at least a few donors who seemed like they could be good candidates.

Michelle didn't stress about the donor being perfect, while I had more reservations. I wondered just how much information we could glean from the sperm bank files. What if he forgot to check a box about his genetic history?

Although I had reservations about my own genes, I did recognize that genetics *and* environment would both create our child. There were no guarantees that our child would turn out anything like the man described online. But it was likely that at least some of his familial history would influence our future kid.

After a thorough review of the best information possible, we felt comfortable and confident in our choice despite the unknowns.

Throughout the process, it was important to keep that choice in perspective. I told myself that there are thousands of women who don't scrutinize their male partner's genetic history before they conceive, and many of those kids turn out fine.

Choosing a sperm donor was a little unsettling. We were choosing the race, ethnicity, and genetic history of our child. This raised ethical questions about how society brings children into this world. We would also get some help from the medical community, by using the IUI technique. But when I stopped to examine the situation, it didn't seem that out of the ordinary. Straight couples and single women can and do use the IUI technique too. When two straight people fall in love or want to create a family, they are also making choices about race, education, and family background, even if those choices are not as explicit or intentional as the ones we were making.

Our top priority was a clean bill of health. The primary reason we chose our donor was that he had few genetic disorders or health issues in his family. Michelle has an uncle living with schizophrenia and several family members who suffer from depression. That, combined with my own family tree, made us want to reduce the probability of mental health issues. We knew there would be no guarantees no matter whom we chose, but I still wanted to create the best possible outcome for my future child. The donor was also described as "good looking" by the sperm bank staff – and that couldn't hurt!

Eventually, Michelle and I chose *Mr. Handsome with a Side of Good Genetics* – at least that's what I called him. He had a professional career and I was attracted to his hand-written essay.

He sounded humble and kind. He recognized that there are people in this world who do not have the ability to create children on their own. He hoped that he could help them in this way. It felt sincere and honest. He also had a good sense of humor. When asked what his advice to prospective parents was, he joked that they shouldn't be too hard on their kid. He seemed like a reasonable guy.

Later, I was surprised to learn that many lesbian mothers we knew, chose a donor because he had the same hair, eye color, or height as one or both the women. In short, they wanted a baby that looked like them.

Having our child look exactly like me was never a top priority. I felt my place. I was the other mother. I'd only be fooling myself if I thought the baby would look like me. I recognized that I would never be genetically related to my child, so my expectations about him or her looking like me were low. Michelle assumed that the kid would look at least a little like her, but it wasn't a priority for her either. She assumed that because she and I looked so similar, any future kids would probably look a little like me too.

At one point, we scrolled over a donor who had a clean bill of health, who also happened to be a redhead. Michelle's aunt, who we were briefly living with at the time, jokingly said "redheads burn easily in the sun." Her former husband was a redhead and both of Michelle's cousins had fare skin. We both gave a little smile and agreed that there might be other, better options. Little did we know, that a different redhead would be entering our lives in less than a year.

Once we committed to the donor we had selected, we tried to maintain flexibility. Some donor sperm can work for one woman while another's may not. We had read that if using a donor's sperm repeatedly, does not result in pregnancy, it may be helpful to choose a different donor or method of insemination. We crossed our fingers, pressed the purchase button online and hoped for the best.

7

ENVY

When Michelle got pregnant, I sometimes felt envious of her pregnancy experience. She was getting all the attention from family and friends. This is when I really started to feel like the other mother. When we would see friends, the pregnancy was all they could talk about.

"Michelle, how are you feeling?"

"Michelle, how are you doing?"

"Michelle, are you excited?"

Michelle, Michelle, Michelle. No one was taking *my* blood, checking *my* hormone levels, or asking about *my* diet. Was I envious that the sperm wasn't in *my* uterus? Probably a little, even after I saw how much pain Michelle experienced during the IUI procedure. Pain was not a common side effect of the procedure, but her uterus was slightly tilted which made it uncomfortable.

The pain was short-lived, so of course *I* could have rocked that out too. It felt like I was standing on the sidelines, while everyone watched and cheered for Michelle. I couldn't help but wonder if this is what straight fathers felt like.

Michelle used to jokingly say, "Stop stealing my thunder." When she was pregnant, if I complained about something, a headache or cramps, Michelle would tell me to get over it.

During the first couple months of pregnancy, she was often sick. I would wake up in the middle of the night to an odd crunching sound, then fall back to sleep. In the morning, I would find stale Cheerios in between the sheets. Apparently, the snacks helped alleviate her nausea. There was no denying that she was sick and deserved my sympathy. But when I happened to have an upset stomach, she basically told me to suck it up. My logical brain told me to stop complaining. But my emotional brain said, what about me?

Had I made the right decision not to get pregnant? Did I want to be pregnant after all? Maybe, someday? With Michelle's growing belly right there in front of me all the time, it was a constant reminder of my choice to be the non-bio mom.

I wondered if the nausea Michelle was feeling or the eventual baby kicks would somehow make her feel more connected to our future baby, than I would. Michelle and the baby growing inside her shared blood and bone – would they also share emotional intimacy in the future, in a different way than me?

As the pregnancy progressed, I tried to better understand where my envy stemmed from. I sat with it. Admitting that the envy came from my own insecurity helped me move through it.

Honestly, it also helped seeing that pregnancy was no cake walk. Michelle once compared being pregnant to having a second job. It took up a lot of time. It took a lot of energy. Even when she would rather be anywhere else than work, she still had to show up in the morning. She still had to be pregnant until she wasn't.

We were relatively lucky though. Michelle had a typical pregnancy, with no medical complications. But by seven months in, she was growing exponentially and experiencing more and more discomfort. She had trouble sleeping, tying her shoes, and zipping up her jacket. I was glad that I wasn't the one having back aches and heartburn. Michelle kept a bottle of Tums on her nightstand and popped them like candy at 4 am.

Feeling the baby kick and squirm was exciting, but a little odd too. From Michelle's perspective, her insides were becoming a punching bag. Michelle would call from the other room of our house, to let me know when the baby was moving. I would hurry, trying get from the kitchen to the living room, to place my hand on her moving belly in time.

"Can you feel it?" she would ask.

"Feel what?" I'd respond. "Oh that?"

The movement was so slight, I thought I felt something, but couldn't totally be sure. It was hard to tell between the baby moving and the gurgling of gas, whose volume and output had multiplied by a thousand. In between the increased belching and flatulence, feeling that little bean inside could be difficult. But as the days and months passed, the baby grew strong!

As first-time parents, we Googled a lot of things. The baby was kicking Michelle's insides so much, that she Googled whether babies could poke holes through a placenta. When Michelle read that babies couldn't do that, I'm not sure she was totally convinced. Sometimes we would joke about baby busting out, and sliding on down the vaginal slide, to life on the outside.

Not feeling the baby move inside *my* womb reinforced my experience as the other mother. I was there physically and emotionally, but as far as the pregnancy symptoms were concerned, they were not happening to me. Toward the end of Michelle's pregnancy, placing my hand upon Michelle's moving belly did make me wonder. *What if that was me? What if I had a baby growing inside of my belly?* On some days, it left me with a longing which I had not previously felt.

Feeling the movements of a living thing was so much different than imagining the what ifs, on that day back at the clinic when Michelle first got inseminated. I didn't know if I was also experiencing hormonal changes or if it was simply because I was in close proximity to a pregnant woman, but I started to think more often, *maybe this could be me someday. And if it wasn't ever going to be me, then would it feel like a loss?* With each passing day, I felt twinges of hopefulness and sadness when I thought about getting pregnant in the future.

Mostly, I tried to step back and appreciate the gift I was receiving. Getting a front row ticket to the big show. For free! I may not have physically felt the pain of the baby kicking, or the acid burning sting of 4 am heartburn, but those experiences were up close and personal.

Watching Michelle go through pregnancy taught me so much. I can't say that I ever completely let go of all the feelings of envy, but they did change. I grew more confident in my own abilities. I recognized that as two people, we were bringing different strengths to the table, just like in our own relationship as partners.

While Michelle was pregnant, I became a great caretaker and for the most part, really enjoyed it. I did the laundry, cooked dinner, and went to the grocery store when the Cheerio box ran empty. When Michelle needed something, I could be there for her. I gave her shoulder massages and tabs of Tums when she asked for them. When Michelle was tired or exhausted, I could be the strong one. This provided a solid foundation for having a positive birth experience. I realized that Michelle and I were going to uniquely contribute to each of our new roles as parents.

8

INVITATION

My mother spent the last decade of her life moving every few years. With each move, she filled large, black trash bags with her belongings. There were even periods where she didn't live in a home at all, but out of a motel room for months at a time. I would think of the motel staff trying to clean her messy room. I imagined the maids trying to vacuum around large piles of paper, saying to themselves, "Oh my god, who is this woman?" I would feel a wave of embarrassment, even though I'd only invented these speakers. Did those houseless periods make my mom *homeless*? After my mom moved into each new place, there was always a grace period before the piles grew large. I wondered if all those moves were my mother's own way of forcing herself to clean.

I recognized that after all these years, while living on my own, I had been trying to protect more than my physical surroundings.

I wasn't living under the same roof as my mother or sister, but I was still bombarded by their constant communication and clutter. If I ever wanted to see my mother, we would meet at restaurants. Go shopping. If I went to her house, there wasn't any clean place for me to sit or stay. She always wanted me to spend the night, but I couldn't stand the newspapers, boxes, and piles of dust. Even taking a drive in her car gave me anxiety, as it too was filled with wrappers, soda cans, papers, and shoes.

After an hour of doing laundry, washing dishes, or and making dinner, all I wanted to do was breathe a sigh of relief and relax. I would turn my cell phone over to check the weather or look at some pictures. Most days of the week, what I had waiting for me was a barrage of text messages or four-minute voicemails from Amy and my mom.

The messages were well-intentioned but confusing. Thoughts leapt from one subject to the next. If I wanted to understand them, I had to decipher the disorganization and misspellings. My sister and mother were both seeking connection, but it felt suffocating. It was like they were constantly inserting themselves into my physical and mental space. I thought about turning off the notifications to my phone, but then I wouldn't be able to hear pings from my friends or Michelle.

I wanted to connect with my mother and sister, but their mental busyness made it difficult. And when Michelle was pregnant, it was the opposite with my dad. We occasionally texted or spoke on the phone, but even in "retirement" he continued to work part-time and I didn't hear from him much. The whole situation left me longing for things to be different.

I saw my mother and sister's energetic spirits. I saw their potential. But when I engaged with them, their disorganization made my own stress flare up.

I used to visit or talk to my mother out of guilt. It was hard not to turn away when she would say:

"Look! I'm here!"

"Talk to me."

"Why don't you want to visit?"

"Why are you seeing your sister and not me?"

I tried to see the good parts too, while also setting more boundaries. I tried to remember the acts of kindness and love, even if they were jumbled with all the rest.

One of the most important lessons I learned from therapy was to do things because I wanted to, not because I felt like I had to. In my twenties, I would get lunch with my mother and feel the taste of resentment in my mouth.

By my early thirties, I had become more selfish. Choosing things because I wanted to, not because I had to. But that's part of becoming a parent, shedding your child-like skin. When you're young, you rely on everyone else to fill your needs, especially your parents. You don't have the tools to make decisions for yourself.

By age 30, I had gained more confidence in my own abilities. I could try to let go of my need for a parent's approval. I had support from myself and my friends. To the best of my abilities, I tried to see my mom as an adult, and act like one myself.

When Michelle was pregnant, I thought about the family I grew up with. A lot. What role would they play when my child was born? How would I share this experience with them, if at all? How had my life changed? Who had I become over the years? What relationship did I want to have with my mother? How could our paths cross when geography and distance divided us? I thought about all the places I had lived, and how my mother was a part of those experiences.

I realized that not once in 15 years, since living on my own, had I *ever* invited my mom into my home.

I thought about it some more. *Was that true?* She had stopped by. We occasionally met up. Went shopping. Ate lunch. But during each of those encounters, we had never hung out inside my house. It was never something we discussed. It's just how it was. If no one points something out as different, then it becomes your normal. I realized how long I had spent pushing my mother away. If I had changed in 15 years, maybe she had too. Maybe our relationship didn't have to be the same one from my childhood.

On the brink of becoming a mother, I thought about my own mortality. How my life would affect my future child's. I started to feel the brevity of our lives. I thought about my mother's life and how few years she probably had left. *How did I want to share those years?*

I decided that I wanted my mom to meet my child after they were born. I imagined her sitting in my living room, holding my baby for the first time. I thought, *I can do that. I can invite her into my house.*

But first, I had to have a trial run.

I booked my mom a hotel room at La Quinta Inn. I was taking a significant risk in the vulnerability department. I wanted to invite her into my home, but I wasn't ready for us to sleep under the same roof.

I bought her a train ticket and asked my sister to print it for her. I went over the directions several times, making sure she knew when, and how to catch the train. My mom was terrible with time. She was notoriously late for everything, so I had to do some prep work.

If my mom and I could get along in the same city for a few days, then I would invite her up again after the baby was born. I texted her throughout the travel day, making sure she was doing okay. She was leaving her comfort zone too. Getting on a train by herself and coming to the big city was an ordeal. My mom lived in rural Oregon, normally a five hour car ride to the Seattle area, or what should have been a six hour train ride.

The train my mom was on, arrived eight hours late at 2 am. I felt terrible.

The journey was already hard enough. My mother was in her seventies, overweight, and still lived with mental health problems. I stood in the dimly lit train station, anxiously waiting her arrival.

When the train car came to a halt, passengers started to exit. Then, a person who looked disheveled and confused stepped onto the platform.

I looked closer.

That person was my mother.

She wore an old worn hat and baggy coat. She shuffled along while pushing a metal luggage cart full of her belongings. At the time, she had a cracked front tooth because she hadn't managed to get herself a dentist appointment. She looked exhausted. But when she saw me, her eyes lit up. We packed her things into the car and headed to the hotel.

At the hotel, we had to wait 20 minutes for someone to check us in. The hotel worker who eventually showed up to the front desk was covered in sweat. He kept wiping his face, but made zero reference to the dripping beads on his brow. I thought, *this is weird. What the hell had he been doing? Working out? Having sex?* Yuck. He looked on the computer screen and handed me a key.

My mom and I made our way to the elevator, then walked down the long hotel corridor. By this time, my mother was walking slowly, her bad legs limping along. I swiped the key card near the door handle. I opened the door and scared some old lady in the dark. I quickly shut the door, and said loudly, "Sorry!" The hotel worker had given me a key that opened an already occupied room.

I found a bench for my mother to sit down on. I went back downstairs and eventually got everything sorted out. I found my mom again. We then found the correct room. I yawned and tiredly said, "See you in the morning." I found the car in the dark parking lot. I drove the few miles back to my house.

The next day, I picked my mom up from the hotel. We went out for a lakeside lunch. She seemed to genuinely appreciate the view. That was something we had in common, a love of moving water – rivers, lakes, the ocean. During my childhood, we had spent many mornings in our family car, parked by the river that ran through downtown. It was something we did before she dropped me off at middle school. I thought that the moving water provided a sense of tranquility to her often busy mind.

After lunch, I drove her around the Kirkland neighborhoods. We then went to a park just north of where we lived. We sat by the water and watched some kids play on the playground. Next, we drove through Snoqualmie Valley to look at the farmland.

The large swaths of open space and trees helped me feel a sense of calm. Afterward, for the first time in my life, I invited my mom to my house. Not just to drive by it, or sit in the yard, but to actually come inside. Instead of inviting her out of guilt, I asked her to come because I wanted her to be there.

We had both changed – at least enough. I had learned to speak my mind more. I didn't need to be afraid of the consequences.

By this time, my mother's age and own experiences had mellowed her out. She still had a challenging time organizing her thoughts and home, but the outbursts and volatility were far less frequent. She sat on our couch, read newspapers, and enjoyed our peekaboo view of the lake.

My mother still wasn't great at actively listening to me, but I could better communicate my boundaries. I made her dinner. I got her a drink of water when she asked. But I could draw the line.

When she requested that we eat random ingredients with dinner, such as "avocados and sweet potatoes," I could have said, and would have said with anyone else, "The store is up the street. You can borrow my car." But that would have been a disaster. She would get lost easily and traffic frightened her. It was difficult, but I learned to say, "No." I could use my voice. When my mother was doing something that bothered me, I tried to respond from a place of compassion instead of annoyance. It didn't always go well, but it went better than it had before.

Over the years, our roles had reversed when we were together. In a lot of ways, I was the parent. I felt like it was my job to take care of my mother, because she couldn't do it herself. But on the precipice of becoming a parent myself, I learned to take a step back. My mother was an adult, even though it didn't seem like it to me sometimes. She was going to do what she wanted. I had to let go of trying to change her or parent her, so that I could become a mother to my own impending child.

Toward the end of my mother's trip, I thought, *This has actually gone well.* We drove along the lake one more time. Ate at a few more restaurants. Sat in my living room and watched the hummingbirds fly by the window. I thought, *Maybe I'm ready for her to meet my child. Maybe I could invite her to visit again. Maybe she could even spend the night inside my house, instead of a hotel.* There were a lot of unknowns, but there had been progress.

On one of my mother's last days, we all went out to the backyard. It was sunny, but cool. Summer had just turned into autumn. The sunflowers I had planted months ago had finally fallen to the ground. We sat on red lawn furniture and Michelle's eight-month pregnant belly bulged. I drank a PBR out of glass bottle. My fingers felt the tiny beads of water, slowly dripping down the side.

I turned toward my mom. She always had her own fashion sense. She wore an extra-large, men's shirt. Red plaid, button-up. Side pony in her hair, askew. She held her hand over her brow, trying to keep the sun from her eyes. It was an appropriate motion to make, but the way her hands were placed looked odd. It was playful and silly. A little ridiculous. Anyone else would have simply asked to borrow a pair of sunglasses.

I felt the slight buzz from lukewarm beer on a new day. I struck the pose too, and asked Michelle to take our picture. My mom and I both smiled, squinting into the sun.

9

BABY NAMES

Some people know right away what they're going to call their child. Michelle and I had a harder time agreeing on a name.

At first, coming up with potential names was fun. We got name ideas from all sorts of places. Even places we didn't expect. We downloaded a few different phone apps that described what was happening to the baby and how it was growing.

With each week that went by, "baby" got bigger and was compared to the size of a food item. Initially, baby was the size of an almond, then an apple, then a squash and so on. Personally, I've never encountered a five-pound papaya, but overall, the app seemed fairly accurate and provided us with a few good laughs. During those first weeks, we fondly called our baby "Poppy," after their initial poppy-seed sized days. As time went on, I went through a "Mr. Babers" phase, but eventually I wanted to give our baby a more culturally appropriate name.

I liked the idea of giving our baby a name that had some familial heritage or geographical significance. Michelle's dad's family emigrated from Ireland, so maybe an Irish name could be a good fit. I had strong feelings for the place I grew up, so perhaps we could name the baby after a northwest mountain range or a pristine lake in Oregon.

Michelle wanted to give our baby a name that met certain criteria. The name had to be mainstream enough to not be considered *weird*, but it also couldn't be *too* popular. This meant the name had to be in the top 1000 most popular names, but not in the top 200. Where did she find the relevant rankings? None other than the Social Security Administration's "Popular Baby Names" website.

I had to admit, the Social Security Administration's baby-name website was incredible. It had statistics on baby names by state, year, gender, and popularity. Michelle was in heaven. Now she had proof on why we should name our baby Finn, which was conveniently already her top pick.

Although I liked the name Finn, I had some reservations. For starters, it felt like all my friend's nephews and dogs had just been given the name. But as Michelle pointed out, Finn really wasn't that popular. In 2015, it was all the way down in 209th place. It wasn't in the top 200! Maybe it was just all those Northwesterners I knew naming their baby Finn. The rest of the U.S. was busy choosing more traditional names like William, James, and Noah (all in the top 10). I started to concede. I put it on the list which was a piece of brown paper bag, stuck to the fridge with a magnet.

As Michelle's pregnancy became more noticeable, people more and more frequently asked what our future baby's name would be. Michelle and I discussed learning about the baby's sex and we both decided we wanted to know. Although we knew that gender would not be chosen by our child until they grew older, we thought that learning the baby's sex would give us a better idea about who he or she might become.

We had learned the baby's sex was male, by doing a genetic blood test at twelve weeks. But simply knowing that fact felt so abstract. I hoped that at Michelle's twenty-week ultrasound I would feel more connected to our child when I saw it move.

The few days preceding the appointment were filled with anticipation. I had seen plenty of movies and knew how this was going to go. I would look at the screen and tears of joy would roll down my face. I would feel a deep connection with the tiny human growing inside my wife.

Michelle and I drove to the appointment together. An assistant showed us to a dimly lit room. When I looked up, there were hundreds of tiny stars painted on the ceiling. I was feeling the magic. Michelle hopped on the table and we waited for the doctor to arrive. When the gel was squirted, and the screen turned on, I was taken aback.

What the hell was I looking at? The creature on the screen looked like a giant lizard. The spinal bones were strongly pronounced. The moving legs looked they belonged to a frog. I did not get teary-eyed. I immediately felt guilty for having had those thoughts.

I had seen plenty of movies with ultrasound images, but our baby's picture seemed different. Perhaps I had seen ultrasounds of a fetus which was older and where the curves of the body looked more human. Seeing the baby move was intriguing, but it didn't make me feel more emotionally connected to him.

Maybe giving our baby a name would help me visualize who he might be or become. I started to rattle off a few names when people inquired. Most of the time, these were met with uninhibited responses. There was something about the baby not being born yet that made people feel like they could let their true opinions fly.

"Eww, I don't like that," someone would say.

"That sounds like a girl's name," their tone implying that we were crazy to suggest giving a girl's name to our *boy*. Or best of all, someone would rattle off all the people (or dogs) they knew with a name I had just suggested.

After having several of these interactions, I went through a phase where I actively avoided baby name talk. If someone asked, I would use deflective tactics and try to steer the conversation elsewhere. But that only worked to a certain degree. People really liked asking about baby names! I got the impression that most people thought talking about baby names was an appropriate, light, topic of conversation. But why did hearing other people's opinions about the names we were considering bother me so much?

Names are complex. Names can have cultural, geographic, and familial significance. Names can also evoke a certain gender. As soon as we started telling people we were going to have a boy, it impacted the conversations we had. Typically, there are boy names and girl names. It felt so binary. It also felt arbitrary. It's just a name, right? But the truth is, a name can shape a person and their experiences.

We all have biases. Seeing or hearing a name for the first time can influence how a person perceives your race or gender. I felt so much pressure to give him the *right* name. I hoped that whatever name we chose, he would feel limitless in his abilities and desires.

When Michelle was pregnant in 2016, there was a trend in naming girls. Many were given what were typically, male first names, or prominent male last names as first names. Examples included Edison, Lincoln, Dylan, Billie, Emmerson, Wyatt, and Elliot. There was a part of me that was excited about this trend-bucking system. When I heard those names, I thought, *how strong*! We should be raising girls who feel strong, powerful, and confident. But what about the boys? It didn't feel like the recent name-game was going in the other direction. Why couldn't there be more *boy* names that were gender-neutral too? I hadn't heard of any baby boys named Harriet, Rose, Linda, Johanna, Curie, or Keller, names typically associated with women or strong female figures.

And what about my future son's last name? That almost seemed like a more important decision than the first name. When my wife and I married, I kept my last name and she kept hers. We were bringing a third person into our family, so what would his last name be? It was something we talked about often. I was already feeling like the "other" mother, did I have to surrender my last name too?

We talked about hyphenation, but we were in strong agreement – there wouldn't be any. We both knew too many people with hyphenated last names that were pronounced incorrectly or all together butchered while we were in school. We wanted to reduce the probability of last name mix ups.

We lightheartedly discussed combining our last names into some sort of mishmash. A friend who was about our age had grown up with two moms. They had given him a combination of both their last names, but it had resulted in something rather obscure. Michelle and I ruled the mishmash out. The one piece of advice from our friend's sister, "Whatever you do, pick something and stick with it." When she was born, her moms' changed their minds after a few weeks. It resulted in a botched birth certificate and several changes to important documents.

We also discussed the possibility of giving our son a totally different last name, unrelated to either of ours. We liked Michelle's mother's maiden name. It also happened to be Michelle's middle name. Michelle's mom kept her last name after she got married to Michelle's father. I liked the idea of keeping some family names, while being non-traditional in their use.

Ultimately, we decided to give our child Michelle's last name. Michelle felt like she identified more with that, than with her mom's last name. To me, Michelle's last name represented all the positive qualities I saw in her family. Drawing from Michelle's own experience and relationship to her mother, my last name became our son's middle name. It didn't feel important to advocate for the last name spot which would be more prominent in its usage. After more consideration, I didn't feel that connected to my last name. I wanted to give him a part of *myself,* not necessarily something associated with my family lineage. Gifting him my last name for his middle name seemed like a way to honor my complex feelings.

Toward the end of the pregnancy, there were so many things to worry about. How were we going to take care of a *baby*? Did we have everything we needed? Had I bought enough diapers, wipes, toys, and everything in between? Did I know enough? We're we prepared enough? I became preoccupied with preparing our baby's arrival to give his first name any more thought.

10

ARRIVAL

Michelle and I had chosen to use a midwife at a hospital birth center shortly after we learned that she got pregnant. It seemed like we would get to experience more one-on-one care with a midwife than with an OB-GYN doctor. Using a midwife at a hospital also reduced our fear about the what ifs. If Michelle needed more medical intervention than what a midwife could offer, we would be geographically close to all the hospital expertise we might need.

We had bonded with our midwife Cate, during months of checkups and appointments. We had learned that she too was part of the queer community. She had become an ally with us on this journey. Over the many appointments that Michelle and I both attended, Cate asked Michelle about her preferences during childbirth to use pain reducing drugs.

Throughout my childhood, my mother took more medications than I could count. They spilled out of her several purses and sat next to our food on the pantry shelf. Although they could have likely helped her, she rarely took them as they were prescribed. My dad also had issues with medication. He suffered from migraine headaches and was prescribed opioid drugs for years. As an adult, I saw the value that medication could bring some people, but mostly saw it as a way to treat symptoms instead of root causes. My childhood perspective still held onto medication being something which tried to fix something that was "wrong." I didn't see anything wrong with the act of childbirth, so my preference was for Michelle to not use any drugs.

Michelle was more open to using pain-relieving drugs, but still wanted to go without. The thought of a needle being placed in her spine was scarier to Michelle than the actual drug effects. Given that it was ultimately her body (and her pain), I would support Michelle in whatever choice she wanted. I did encourage her to stick to the *preferences* and not have an epidural. Either way, we agreed to stay the course.

It was early October and it officially felt like fall. The previous weekend, one of our good friends from Portland had just visited. We made a trip to the pumpkin patch, and took pictures in between the downpours. It was hard not to compare Michelle's bulging belly, to the giant orange orbs that littered the ground.

It was on the following Saturday that my wife and I went to bed at 10 pm, but awoke a brief two hours later. Michelle's fingers pulled at my shoulder and I groggily heard whispers in my ear. I looked over in the dark at my phone – it read 12 am.

"I think I wet the bed," she said.

"Wait, what?" I shook off my sleepiness and turned on the bedside lamp.

"The bed is all wet."

"Maybe your water broke."

Michelle got up to use the bathroom. Liquid continued to trickle down her legs.

"What color is the liquid?" I asked. We were in a state of surprise, given that Michelle's due date was still almost three weeks away. We thought we had plenty of more time for planning and preparing. Michelle seemed to be in a complete state of denial, assuring herself, me, and the air, that she had simply lost her abilities to control her bladder. When I expressed suspicion, she said, "Smell it." I wrinkled my nose in response.

Weeks earlier, we had taken a birthing class where we learned that amniotic fluid would be clear and odor free, while urine was darker and more aromatic. I took a small whiff of the liquid.

"I'm pretty sure your water broke," I said.

Michelle was *still* not totally convinced.

It felt like something we *should* know. If we couldn't tell if we were having a baby, were we really *ready* for a baby?

I let out a breath, releasing the nerves buzzing inside me. "We should definitely call the nurse hotline." I was trying to step into my caretaker role, the one I had carved out over the last nine months. I picked up the phone. I found the number which I had previously stored in my phone's contact list. First name, *Birth*. Last name, *Center*. I dialed Ms. Birth Center and a receptionist answered the phone. We briefly chatted. She reinforced my suspicions and told us to come in.

We grabbed our to-go hospital bag and hopped in the car. My humming nerves had returned. *Could this be it? Are we ready? How long will it take?* Questions floated in and out of my mind. I parked the car in the appropriate hospital *visitor* parking space. Before I closed the car door, I looked in the back seat. We had remembered to bring the baby car seat and I wondered if the next time I saw it, there would be a *baby* sitting inside it.

At this point, Michelle was not in pain, but the liquid between her legs continued to flow. Michelle sat in a lobby chair. "Isn't there a place we can go?" I asked. The receptionist made a phone call, then a nurse took us through the double doors. We made our way to a bathroom. Michelle was given some thick, paper-like underwear and a giant maxi pad. "Ooo, sexy," I joked.

We left the bathroom and Michelle was asked to lie on a table in a nearby room. A baby heart monitor was placed on her belly. The nurse proceeded to check how far Michelle's cervix was dilated. She donned the rubber gloves and pressed on various parts of Michelle's body. My wife gasped in agony. It was hard not to yell at the nurse, "Stop! You're hurting her!" But I kept my thoughts to myself, knowing that there was far more pain to come.

The birth journey had begun! We were told that because Michelle's water had broken, we could either continue to stay at the hospital or go home. Her cervix was only dilated one centimeter. If we left, we were supposed to return within 12 hours or whenever the pain became too much. *Twelve hours?!* That seemed far, far away.

ARRIVAL

We were still feeling giddy with excitement and chose to leave. Michelle figured she would feel more comfortable at home than inside of a hospital room. I wanted as much time as possible outside the hospital to mentally prepare myself for what was going to come next, so I was okay with heading home too.

We hadn't expected to have a baby for several more weeks, so we were unprepared in the food department. Our fridge was practically empty. Everyone had told us that having a stocked pantry when the baby came was a good idea. At 2 am we headed to the 24-hour grocery store. We wandered the store, largely empty of customers, and shopped the *Discount Dairy* sales. We filled the basket with our favorite foods. We picked up some baby shampoo because we had yet to buy any. But after a few more trips up and down the aisles, Michelle's contractions started to intensify. We quickly hurried to the check-out, then hopped in our Prius and headed home.

Somewhere along the way, we had read that the pregnant mama should eat a lot during labor. Our thinking was, Michelle was about to complete a marathon, so she should carbo load. I imagined feeding granola bars to Michelle, while she labored along. At one point we mentioned this to our midwife during a monthly checkup, and she respectfully chuckled. I remember not quite getting the joke, but it would soon be clear.

Between contractions, Michelle calmly ate a small burrito, when no more than 10 minutes later, she proceeded to throw up the contents of her stomach into our toilet bowl. The joke was on us. The contractions continued to increase in intensity and length. Around 5 am, she decided it was too much and we headed back to the hospital.

The second time we went to the hospital, we were prepared to stay – at least until we were holding a baby in our arms. Michelle's cervix was checked for a second time that morning. Even though the pain had increased, her cervix was only dilated two centimeters. I had expected it to be way more than that. Michelle changed into a gown, was hooked up to more monitors, and was told to lie on the bed. We were then told that our primary midwife, Cate, was not on call. My heart sank. There was only one other midwife in the practice.

We had assumed that the odds of Cate being available when Michelle delivered were high. I had created an image of how this birth journey would go, and she was supposed to be in it. But in the words of Cate, "You don't call it a *Birth Plan*, you call it *Birth Preferences*."

A nurse came in to check on us. "I'm so excited to be a part of an NCB!" she said.

"NCB? What is that?" I asked.

"Natural Child Birth," she responded.

Apparently, we were participating in not only a birthing experience, but a medical acronym.

It turned out that although Cate was not on call, she was in the hospital. When she entered our room, I felt relieved to see her. She said she had promised a pregnant trans patient that she would deliver their baby. A flood of thoughts ran through my mind. This is why I liked Cate. She valued her patients. She came to the hospital on her day off, went out of her way to check on us, and communicated with our nurses. I held an inward smile, thinking, *what are the odds? A trans and lesbian patient go into labor on the same day?*

Cate saw Michelle lying on the hospital bed and gave her permission to stand up and walk around. I appreciated her small, but meaningful gesture for patient advocacy. I glanced out the hospital window to see a cloudy day and rain pouring down. The wind was slapping water onto the hospital windows. Cate said with a smile, *"Nothing like a storm to bring in the pregnant people."*

Before she left, Cate said we were in good hands with the on-call midwife, Lana. We had met Lana before, at a couple brief appointments. Although neither Michelle nor I felt a deep connection with her, she seemed professional and knowledgeable.

It was midday before Michelle's cervix started to open in earnest. Her contractions had been about two minutes apart for the past nine hours. We were both exhausted, running on only two hours of sleep. Michelle felt like there were no breaks in between the bouts of pain. She rolled over, lay on her side, threw up, and the cycle repeated. I heaped words of encouragement and praise into the air. I massaged her tensing muscles.

Michelle had originally been so excited about the soaking tubs she saw in the hospital pamphlet. After 20 minutes of filling the tub and lighting candles, I helped slide her large body into the warm water. I crossed my fingers that this would bring some relief. But after only two minutes, she was up and out. It was more painful to lie still, than to move her shaking body.

Michelle was in pain, and I needed to provide support – that was my job. Her doubts about her birthing abilities became more frequent. "I can't do this," she would say. But I tried my best to be steady and continue providing emotional support. I did not waver in my confidence of her. Over and over again, I said, "You *can* do this. You're doing great!" I tried to keep it simple and to the point.

But I was also increasingly growing tired too, though attempting to *stay strong*. I admitted to myself that I needed a break. A nurse mentioned that there was a fully stocked pantry in a nearby kitchen for patients.

I stepped out of our room, walked down the hall, and grabbed a sandwich from the fridge. I brought it back to the room and tried to hurriedly eat it in the corner. Michelle spied me from her perch and snapped, "Get back here! I need my back massaged." To this day, this is one of our favorite recounts of the birth; me, sandwich in hand, trying to catch a break, while Michelle was not shy about her needs.

By 5 pm, we were in the thick of it. Lana was there, changing her gloves every five minutes, while Michelle let loose a cascade fluids. Michelle had endured more than 12 hours of pain, with limited drug intervention. She did not take an epidural, but did end up receiving some pain relief through an IV. It only took the edge off for a two-hour period, but it was enough time that I could sneak in a few more bites of sandwich.

Finally, Lana said that Michelle could push. I was instructed to brace myself while holding one of Michelle's feet. I thought, *Brace myself on what?!* This was not a job they discussed in our birthing class. Michelle continued to push, and became high on endorphins (and possibly that previous IV drip). When Lana asked her a question or simply provided praise, Michelle would respond in a sarcastic, harsh tone, "This is America. I should have taken the drugs," lamenting her choice to not take the epidural.

At one point, the three of us were squeezed into the dark bathroom, and Michelle said, "I want to have this baby right now!"

Lana responded, "I promise you, you will not have your baby on the toilet."

Michelle said, "I would *love* to have this baby on the toilet!"

These humorous moments provided some relief from the intensity of the situation. But, there was also a nagging apprehension that started to creep inside me. *When the baby came, would Michelle be able to overcome her pain and bond with the baby? Would I be able to connect to him too?*

My mind leaped back in time to that twenty-week ultrasound. The one where all I could see, was an odd-looking lizard baby. I tried to push the image out of my mind and focus on the task at hand, getting that baby *out*.

Through it all, there was progress. Our son's head finally started to crown. I remember thinking, *Maybe our boy isn't that large.* He had measured large on the ultrasound. But in that moment, when Michelle was pushing, our son's head looked small. But with each push, I started to see more and more. It turned out, the baby's head was squeezing into a cone-like shape, so it could fit through the small opening. I had previously learned this, but was still very surprised to see my son's giant head, eventually push through all at once. Once the head came, so did the rest. When I saw that white, gunky covered baby, I thought, *Oh my god, what have we done?* I did not instantly fall in love with the baby before me.

Part of me was stunned. This baby did not look like as I had imagined. He did not look like the babies on TV or in magazine photographs. I felt a little repulsed. I then immediately felt guilty. Why did I not feel connected to him? Michelle looked beyond exhausted. *How was she going to react to our son, now that he was here?* She just lay there looking miserable.

In matter of minutes, the nurses wiped down our baby. He had gained a pinkish, more human-looking hue, and was placed on Michelle's chest.

She then bent down and kissed his head.

Internally, I let out a giant sigh of relief. Everything was going to be okay. I could let go of the anxiety and the adrenaline that had been coursing through my veins all day. We could finally rest. I simply watched the two of them for several minutes, and softly stroked the baby's head.

Then the baby started to turn white again, his breath slowed, his coos quieted. I became worried. Michelle was too exhausted to notice. I alerted a nurse who scooped him up. She placed him under some warming lights and he began to scream. In a few short minutes, he regained his color again.

I would look back on that moment, recognizing that although my connection to my son was not instantaneous, it was there from the beginning, lightly building into something fierce. I would always be there to protect my son – trying my best to keep him safe.

After our son's initial entrance, and the little scare, it turned out that our son was extremely cute. What a transformation a few minutes could make.

We had all done our part. I had never been prouder of anyone before that day. Michelle had worked physically harder than anyone I had ever seen. She had shown more mental perseverance than anyone I knew. Our son had completed his journey from womb to outside world. I had provided the emotional and physical support I wanted to give.

We made our way to a new hospital room. It was clean. It was quiet. We spent our first night together as a family. When the final nurse went to leave, I think it struck us both. We were right where we wanted to be. We had been preparing for the moment for over a year – deciding who would get pregnant, choosing the sperm donor, seeing the positive pregnancy test, and going to all those pregnancy appointments.

There was a moment of calm. Michelle and I both took turns holding our new baby. We felt his warmth and looked into his eyes. When my son came out a redhead, the name *Finn* initially felt right – it felt true to his Irish ancestry. However, I still wanted his name to be unique. I wanted his name to evoke kindness, confidence, and strength. I wanted to buck the name giving trend, even if it was only in the slightest of ways.

We decided on his full name together. His full, first name would be one that is also given to girls. *Finnley.*

We continued to hold our little baby in our arms. We felt the weight of his life in our hands. The moment had finally arrived. We were parents.

11

JACKPOT

Having a redhead, is the equivalent of winning the parenting jackpot.

Having a redhead is cool. Having a redhead is an anomaly. Everyone notices. Our kid gets *a lot* of attention. As a parent, it was like being part of an exclusive club.

Other redheads stopped me at the grocery store to admire my son's hair. The conversations sometimes verged on being too intimate, but by and large, the interactions were casual. People would say things like, "Oh, your baby has red hair too?" or "My hair used to be that color when I was a kid." I turned to them and usually responded simply, "Yeah. Cool." as I nodded my head in agreement.

Sometimes they would say, "Does his dad have red hair?"

Initially this question made me uncomfortable. I am a terrible liar. I don't like lying. But describing all the reasons why Finnley didn't have a "dad" just didn't seem right, especially when I was speaking with strangers.

After six months of having Finnley in public, I finally developed enough confidence to give brief and vague answers to questions that made me feel uncomfortable. When someone asked about where his red hair came from, I'd typically say something like, "It just runs in the family," or my favorite, "We feed him a lot of carrots."

Even if you swapped out the red hair for blonde or brown, he still doesn't look more like Michelle than me. Only people we have told, know that Finnley is biologically related to Michelle. It's like we have something special that we get to hold onto. We get to decide who to tell and how.

Learning when and how to out myself as his non-biological parent wasn't always easy. When others commented about his looks, it initially caused me to feel insecure, because I assumed they were thinking he didn't look like me. But in time, I learned to navigate social situations and questions with more confidence. I learned that having answers on hand, already prepared, could go a long way. The answers helped me feel more confident about my role as a parent and set boundaries related to my non-biological parental status.

12

FINDING SUPPORT

Michelle and I joined two parenting groups shortly after Finnley was born. In the Seattle area, there was an organization that had recently added a parenting group specifically catering to the queer community. From Ballard to Burien, Mercer Island to Kirkland, members lived throughout the Seattle-metro region. Shortly after joining the "Queer Group," we also joined what we dubbed, the "Straight Group." Unlike Queer Group which spanned across Seattle and beyond, Straight Group was neighborhood-based.

In both groups we had open discussions about how to do basic things, like when to start feeding solid foods or how to put your baby to sleep.

The first time we went to Straight Group, I felt out of place. It was an evening meeting, which meant it took place when our son and all the other babies usually slept. We drove in the dark, looking for the host's house. Finnley was cranky. We were already running on fumes from our own lack of sleep. We walked up to the porch and rang the doorbell. A perky woman in her mid-30s let us in. She was the group's facilitator.

As soon as we sat down, it was obvious that her whole lesson plan revolved around each kid having a mom and a dad. She went around, asking each couple a few questions. When she made her way to us, she was a deer in the headlights. We were the only gay parents in the room. There weren't any adoptive or single parents either. I was trying to shoot her telepathic thoughts to *act cool. You don't have to point out that our son has two moms, it's obvious.* I tried not to get defensive when she asked, "Which one of you stays home with the baby?" But I did, and mentally rolled my eyes.

In this busy world, you are lucky if you get two weeks off work after you give birth, and doubly lucky if you get paid for it. You are triple lucky if your partner can take parental leave. At the time, I was working for a small business. As the non-bio mom, I received zero paid time off after my wife gave birth. The facilitator seemed blind to any of these issues. Secondly, her question implied that if there were two women taking care of a baby, *clearly* one of them must be playing homemaker.

I was offended – but in a split-second, I decided to tell the truth. I was still learning when to tell, and what to tell. In doing so, I outed myself as Finnley's non-biological parent. I said, "Michelle gave birth to our son. And fortunately, her job allows three months for maternity leave. I'm currently working full-time."

I wish I would have answered differently.

My answer showed that I felt defensive – that I saw myself as the second parent, not an equal. That I believed it mattered which one of us gave birth to our son.

After that, I was rather judgmental about Straight Group based on how the initial meeting had gone. *Suburbanites.* Boring. Run of the mill mommies and daddies. They worked for Microsoft, Amazon, Expedia. Your typical East Side techies. But secretly, I was envious of their parental leave, big houses, and lucrative jobs.

You can throw a bunch of people into a room together, but if they don't have shared values or similar interests, it can be hard to develop meaningful relationships. Also, taking care of a baby is all consuming. In those early days, if you didn't live within 15 minutes of my house, I probably wasn't going to see you. That was one thing the Straight Group did have going for it. We all lived relatively close to one another.

Over the next couple months, I went on a few coffee baby-dates with some of the Straight Group mothers. I learned where they lived, what they did for work, and what some of their hobbies were. We didn't share deep conversations, but it did bring us closer together. It was selfishly helpful to have a listening ear during those most difficult and stressful months of parenthood.

I started to see the couples' positive qualities. There was humor. Kindness. And the willingness to help. When Michelle and I had to move out of our rental because the house got sold, some of the parents came over to load our boxes into the U-Haul. After that, I felt guilty for my previous judgements and categorizations.

Joining Queer Group started on a humorous note. Having arrived early, Michelle and I decided to wait in the car for a few minutes before entering the host's house. Finnley was a few months old and had fallen asleep while driving. I looked over at Michelle, sitting it the passenger seat.

I turned to her and jokingly asked, "How many other *Finns* do you think there will be?"

"I bet there will be one other," she said with a smile on her face.

Finnley stirred in his car seat, waking up with a tiny yawn. It was time to go in.

I rang the doorbell and the meeting host let us in. While kicking off my shoes, I introduced myself. I said, "I'm Lora. This is my wife Michelle, and our son Finnley."

She turned to me and said, "No way!" I looked at her with a slightly puzzled expression.

"No way, what?" I asked.

"You're the *third* Finnley to arrive," she responded.

Out of five boys present, three of them were named Finley. Not just Finn, but *Finley*! Granted, their names only had one "*n*" instead of two, but still, I was a little shocked. I thought I had given our son a unique name. It seemed like Finn was popular, but *Finnley*?

I guess my previous notions about the name Finn, were correct. Although, to this day, I still haven't met a boy named *Finley* or *Finnley* with straight parents. Michelle and I joked with one another about the name being like a secret code. We imagined our son as a teenager, meeting someone with the same name.

"Hey there. What's your name?" our son would ask.

"My name is Finnley. Nice to meet you," the other boy would respond.

"Your name is *Finnley*? That's my name!"

They would look at one another and say in unison, "You must have two moms too!"

The queer parents I met were as diverse as the rainbow flag, fluttering at Pride. One couple at the Queer Group shared that he was a trans man and introduced his female partner. Another couple was comprised of two femmes, one of whom used her partner's egg and donated sperm, also known as reciprocal IVF.

A lesbian in her mid 40s had just given birth to her second child. She had used a donated sperm *and* egg, from the same donors, for both births. Thus, neither she nor her wife had any genetic relation to their children, but the children were biologically related siblings.

One couple consisted of a white woman and a woman of Hawaiian-Asian descent, and they told their story of how hard it was for the latter to find an Asian donor's sperm. One couple searched multiple sperm banks for a Jewish donor. Each couple's story was unique, and somewhere we fit into the mix. Family trees branched in every direction.

The parent I felt most connected to was named Jennie. Jennie and her wife had a son only a few days older than Finnley. During one of the meetings, the facilitator asked all the parents about what was currently difficult at home. All of our babies were about five months old.

When it came to Jennie's turn, she said, "I just hope that my son likes me." There was a collective exhale from all the parents in the room.

"Of course he will," we all chimed in.

In that moment, I felt like Jennie and I shared similar feelings of insecurity, especially during the beginning months of parenthood.

About a year after our initial meeting, Jennie and I were still in contact and met up for a beer. I asked her, "When do you most feel like the *other mother*?"

Jennie is a woman of few words. But when she speaks, it is to the point. She has a cutting, dry sense of humor which appears out of nowhere. With a smile on her face, she responded, "Well, my wife is still breastfeeding."

Her son was 17 months old at the time. Jennie said that her son was not likely getting much milk, but that her wife was not ready to give up the bonding experience. Admittedly, she wondered aloud why her wife still insisted on the practice, just like I had (Michelle eventually stopped breastfeeding, when Finnley was 19 months old). Jennie and I both recognized that it was up to our wives to decide when to stop, but it was hard not to question why they continued the practice when the children didn't *need* the milk anymore. We spoke of the situation quietly, almost like we were guilty to express such thoughts. But our partners were not there. We were free to vocalize our questions and wonders.

Out of all the things that made me feel inadequate or like I was the other mother, breastfeeding may have been the largest. It was a mystery that I would never know. But unlike pregnancy which I didn't experience either, my son was an active participant during breastfeeding. When Finnley cried, Michelle could soothe him in a way I couldn't. She literally gave herself to him for nourishment. As a non-active participant, I could appreciate the power and vulnerability that the act of breastfeeding possesses. But I also deeply felt the lack of ability to connect with my son in the same way as my wife.

I had briefly thought about breastfeeding Finnley too. I had read about non-bio moms taking hormones to stimulate milk production. But given my aversion to drugs in general, I wasn't that interested. But to just be sure, I took off my shirt one time to see if breastfeeding was something Finnley or I wanted to do together. It wasn't. The pain I felt was sharp and surprising. I quickly redressed and gave Finnley to Michelle for his next meal.

The other topic that Jennie mentioned was how others perceived her. Specifically, straight men. Jennie had short cropped hair and dressed casually. Pants and button-down shirt. She described herself as not being masculine, but being perceived in that way by her male friends. When Jennie and her male friends hung out in a group, some of them spoke to her like she was "one of the guys." They assumed because she was the non-bio mom, that her role was like theirs, that of a stereotypical dad. One who tried to get out of his responsibilities or nagged about his wife behind her back. But Jennie expressed that's not how she felt. She tried to describe to her guy friends that she and her wife split responsibilities equally. That there were more similarities in their roles than there were differences.

I too felt the sharing of responsibility with Michelle. As a two-mom family, we had carved out our family unit to be equal in our parental roles. For example, we both maintained professional careers while raising Finnley. We both changed diapers, played with our son, and did laundry. When Michelle and I looked at some straight couples we knew with kids, we saw a different picture. It looked like mom and dad roles were split differently. Typically, dad focused on his career, while mom stayed home to care for the children. Not all of our straight friends subscribed to this, but certainly some. And I didn't see or hear resentment from mom or dad. Part of me envied these distinct roles because I wondered if it was easier than trying to make things *equal*. When Finnley was young, I returned to that thought often. Eventually, I recognized that not all responsibilities like breastfeeding would be equal in me and Michelle's relationship – because they simply couldn't be. I was never going to breastfeed.

After the three-month-long Queer Group ended, we stayed in touch with a few families and occasionally met with the larger group for gatherings like birthdays, holidays, or Seattle Pride.

I will always be grateful that we found the Queer Group because it validated our story. It validated *my* story. I wasn't alone. There were other mothers in similar positions as me. There were queer, non-bio moms who were also asking questions about their parental roles and expressing concerns that they felt like the *other* mother.

13

CONTROL

Control went out the window when a baby entered my life. Babies do what they want. When they want.

The unknown used to be scary. I tried to control things because I feared the consequences of leaving decisions in someone else's hands. While growing up, I never knew what to expect at home. My mother might be acting fine one moment, but then get in a catastrophic argument the next. I would escape to my room as I heard her fists pound on the table. If I couldn't physically leave, then I had to claim control where I could.

I became self-sufficient. My family didn't do things the way I wanted, so I improvised. I took control of my life; I put myself in the driver's seat. If I wanted a home cooked meal, instead of Domino's Pizza, I made it. If I wanted to get myself to basketball practice on time, I drove myself. Those habits served me well for a time. I graduated high school and college, built community, went to grad school, and traveled near and far. But, I had also gotten stuck in my ways.

I thought that if I planned enough, I could control the outcome. I would lie in bed at night, having conversations in my head, with someone I was slated to see the following day. I would plan an evening, to watch a specific movie and eat a certain flavor of ice cream. But I would fail to mention this plan to the person whom I shared the night with. Sometimes it would all work out and I would get what I wanted. But other times, it didn't.

When my expectations failed to pan out, I felt severely disappointed. Because my plans and expectations didn't always leave my head, sometimes this resulted in miscommunications and hurt feelings.

Michelle showed me that it's okay if something goes differently than you anticipate. The world will not end because the salad has a chopped carrot instead of a shredded one. I started to accept that having fewer expectations about life opened me to the possibilities of new and exciting experiences. But that didn't happen before Michelle and I had many conversations about what a "reasonable" expectation looks like. It seems so obvious now, but it took me a long time to get there.

When I didn't have expectations, good things could happen. It felt like the world was throwing me a surprise party, and I was the guest of honor. But being a planner and letting go of control was hard. I knew this firsthand. I had devoted a lot of energy toward trying to let go, and I saw the irony in that.

I knew that being a parent would be filled with a lot of unknowns. I knew that I was going to have to continue letting go of control. A newborn is completely helpless and relies solely on its caregivers. Our son didn't know what time of day it was, how to eat, or even how to sleep. He had to learn *everything*. Parenting was all-consuming: changing diapers, doing laundry, and cleaning spit-up off the couch. I had no idea how much time I would end up wiping pee from all of our surfaces – the changing table, the bathmat, the bedroom carpet too. I had to let go of having a supremely organized house. I had to let the dirty pots and pans sit on the counter for an extra hour or two, or even for an entire day! And more importantly, there was also the emotional energy like rocking, soothing, and staying calm while the baby wailed.

Michelle was frequently as exhausted as I was, but she was far more patient. When our son was in a biting phase, she rarely raised her voice at him – even after he bit her nipple, multiple times. I wondered how she did it. *Was it her innate personality? The way her brain perceived the situation?*

I did not voice it, but I wondered if it was because she was his biological mother. *Did they have a connection that my son and I didn't?* I learned to try to not dwell on the whys. It didn't really matter why – it only mattered how I acted. What I did with my frustrations and how I interacted with my child. When I felt frustrated over the lack of control, I had the ability to decide what to do with it.

Being a new parent felt overwhelming. I had expected the sleepless nights, but actually living them was far different than anything I could have imagined. It was difficult to experience sleepless nights, then get up and go to my full-time job. Because we had moved relatively recently to Washington, I had taken a random job with a land surveying company. The job was physically demanding and I had to be at work by 6:30 am. A few months after Finnley was born, I eventually got a job more in my field, as the manager of a local farmers market. But those first few months of Finnley's life were difficult. My parents were not going to be caretakers or an extra set of hands for our newborn. Michelle's parents helped some, but they lived in Bellingham, about a two hour drive away with traffic. Although we eventually established some connections with people in the Straight and Queer Groups, we had little community support in the first few months directly after Finnley's birth.

The sleep deprivation affected my mood. My emotional well-being. My physical well-being. My mental well-being. It was the cause of conflict between me and Michelle. And who I became in the middle of the night, made me wonder if I was turning into my own mother.

Sleeping (or lack thereof), was hands-down, the hardest thing about being a parent in those early days. During the first few months of Finnley's life, I struggled. Exhaustion got the best of me. With each bout of crying, I would become angrier. I'd vacillated between holding it together and losing it. Sometimes I'd raise my voice, storm off to the next room, or snap at Michelle. It felt as if the night turned me into a different person.

It was 3 am and I had been awakened for the third time in one night. Finnley, was eight weeks old. That's how I knew he was young. We didn't count his age in years or months. We counted them in *weeks*.

I was waking to his cries every two hours. A coworker was gracious enough to give me his cold, which I then passed on to my baby. Michelle was angry with me, as she saw me as the culprit who had made her baby miserable. I felt the guilt of a parent who got her baby sick. Every small ill felt giant. When I took him to the doctor, she said it could take up to four weeks before the cold ran its course.

"Four weeks!" I exclaimed, as I tried not to show too much surprise. *That's half of the amount of time he has been outside the womb,* I thought. The days of taking care of a healthy baby already seemed to tick by slowly. The thought of caring for an increasingly agitated, cranky, and sick baby felt daunting. I left the doctor's office feeling defeated. *Four weeks?* As I carried Finnley to the car I whispered in his ear, "Let's hope it's only two."

When I got back home, Finnley was stuffy and had trouble breathing. He didn't know how to blow his nose. He didn't know how to sleep. He didn't even know if it was day or night. I reminded myself he had to learn how to do *everything*. He only weighed a little more than a ten-pound bag of potatoes. I cycled between cradling him and carefully placing him on my chest. There was little I could do.

I took Finnley out of our bedroom. I remembered the doctor saying that steam from a shower could help clear his nose. I was doubtful it would help, but I felt so exhausted. I would do anything or try anything for the promise of more sleep.

I went to the bathroom, turned on the water, and sat on the cold lid of the toilet. Finnley wailed. I placed his ear on my chest, encouraging him to hear the steady beat of my heart. I breathed in the steam too. I also had a stuffy head, snot running from my nose, and a sore throat. The warmth of the steam loosened my muscles and I started to get drowsy. But then I told myself, *wake up!*

Eventually Finnley's cries dissipated. I tried to put him back in the sleeper in our bedroom. He let out another cry, clearly wanting to be held instead of being left alone. I scooped him back up and headed for the living room. I sat on the sofa, propped up by back, and laid Finnley upright on my chest. He felt so tiny and fragile. I felt even more tired than before, but I fought the urge to close my eyes, fearing I might fall asleep and drop him. The thought of him tumbling to the floor with a thud, gave me the little adrenaline boost I needed. My eyes opened. I was awake.

The first time my wife told me to "stop yelling at the baby," my heart sank. It was nighttime. The curtains were closed. It was dark. "Was I really yelling?" I asked? My insecurities were instantly heightened. I was ashamed. I was brought back to my childhood. "Yelling" in my family meant loud shouting matches in public. That's not what I had done. I was a little confused about the semantics, but mostly, I felt like I let my wife and son down. I was disappointed in myself and it felt like my worst nightmares were coming true. I did not have the necessary skills to take care of my baby.

Michelle was the angriest she had ever been with me. Interacting with the baby *appropriately*, specifically at night, and when he cried, became one of our biggest topics of conversation. Not in its frequency, but in its weight. Michelle wanted me to be more nurturing and kind. If we tried to have the conversation when tension was high, and Finnley was crying, I would think, *this is the best I can do.*

Michelle told me I had to figure out how to change my behavior. It got so bad at one point, that Michelle said it made her wonder whether we could handle having a second kid. I was devastated. When we revisited the topic, months later, Michelle was still shaken by how I had behaved. Her words stung. *Was I really that bad?* I asked myself. My fears of being a terrible parent were coming true.

I tried to consider what should be acceptable parenting behavior. When Michelle said I was "yelling" at the baby, I paused in disbelief. *Yelling?* Yelling is screaming at the top of your lungs. It's violent. These were the definitions and images I had held onto since childhood. I wasn't doing that. But I knew I was doing *something* wrong. I felt it.

I didn't like being that angry person in the middle of the night. I was making my wife uncomfortable. And it certainly wasn't positive, loving behavior I was showing my son. I continued to feel embarrassed and ashamed. It took an outsider's perspective to change my perception. Even though my behavior wasn't extreme, it had to change.

When I was by myself and calm, I'd let Michelle's words sink in. *I could do better*, I thought. I asked myself, *Do I have the skills to take care of this child before me? Am I good enough parent? How can I do better?*

Although Michelle was angry, she also exuded patience and kindness - not all the time, but more frequently than me. Sometimes it was maddening. *Why doesn't the baby's crying affect her in the same way? Is it just who she is? Or is it because she is the biological mother?* Even though she was upset, she continued to support me. She created a list of things that I could do when I felt frustrated. When I had to calm myself and let go of control, some options were: sing a song, create a distraction, take a breath, speak kindly. She took out a ballpoint pen and wrote the four suggestions down in a bulleted list. The small scrap of paper hung near the changing table for a year. I knew it was my job to teach my son how to develop healthy behaviors. I thought, *those behaviors must start with me.*

When Finnley was a few months old, I started to sleep in our spare bedroom on occasion. At the time, Finnley was still only breastfeeding and not taking bottles, so there wasn't much I could do in those moments when he was hungry. I had waited to sleep in the spare room because I didn't want to feel like a failure. I wanted to feel like I could do it all. But as the non-bio parent who was not breastfeeding, there simply was no way I could do it all.

What I realized, was that sleep made me a "good parent." In fact, it made me a *better* parent. It also made me a better partner. With more rest, I could more appropriately respond to Finnley's needs in the daytime and nighttime which helped our family unit.

In the daytime too, sometimes I simply needed a break. I would hand Michelle our screaming son, and walk into the next room. I would later go for a walk around the block, or to the store, and let my mind wander. *How can I do it better the next time? How can I stay calm, even when Finnley bites my neck or hits me in the face?* While aimlessly walking the produce isle, I'd tell myself that he is a child and I am his parent. I knew I had to model the behaviors I wanted see in him. As a parent, I had to embrace being a teacher. Over, over, and over again, I taught the same things to my son and hoped that he learned something new. And as I taught, I, too, embraced my new found skills.

14

JUST CALL ME MOM

My son has two moms. It's obvious. Right? When I look at myself and my wife, I think: *We definitely look gay*. Especially when we're standing next to one another. It's not just about our physical appearance, but it's how we interact with each other. It's how we carry ourselves. But sometimes our relationship as gay women, wives, and mothers was not apparent to the rest of the world.

As the second parent, I frequently outed myself twice in a conversation. The first time, I outed myself as gay. The second time, as the non-biological mother. I could live in the closet and never tell anyone about my personal life – but that's not practical. And it's simply not me. I'm also privileged to be living in the relatively gay-friendly Northwest. But having to decide who to tell, what to tell, and when to tell, made for some awkward situations.

When Finnley was young, we took a trip to attend Michelle's brother's wedding. It took us a few flights to get there, and when we returned, I tried my best to get through airport security as quickly as possible. I held Finnley in my arms as I stood in the lengthy line. I attempted to take off my shoes and belt, while heaving my belongings onto the luggage belt. The process somehow felt rushed and slow at the same time. We finally made our way to the front of the line. Then out of nowhere, someone in a navy blue uniform asked to do a special scan of the stroller we had brought. I just wanted to get the process over with, so I could catch my overpriced flight back home.

The security guard, a young guy in his twenties, said, "Yo. Are you two, like, *twins*?" He looked from me to Michelle. "You look *so* similar!" he said with a big grin on his face, like we were part of the joke.

I wanted to yell, "No! She is not my sister. She is my wife!" But I kept my cool. He was probably just trying to spice up his dull daily routine. I kept my comments to myself, hoping he would just drop the topic. Later, I thought, we have all done this before. Made assumptions about people which turn out not to be true.

Only ten minutes before, we had a vastly different encounter. We were riding an airport tram, crammed alongside a bunch of other people. I tried to keep my balance by holding the metal bar, while also holding Finnley. Michelle oversaw the luggage. Next to us, was a mother (I assumed) and her three young children. We exchanged chit chat while the tram bumped along. As the door slid open, we stepped onto the platform to leave. The mother said to her kids, "Let the moms go first." I mentally noted how she had made the word *mom*, plural. She recognized us as two parents, without us ever overtly outing ourselves. Two people could see the same situation, but come to vastly different conclusions.

Like the facilitator in Straight Group, many people whom I didn't know well, would ask me which one of us gave birth to Finnley. In the beginning, I'd ask myself: How much do I say? What do I tell them? Why do they assume that either of us gave birth to him at all? It took me about a year after Finnley was born to gain confidence in giving the answers I genuinely wanted to provide.

I understood the curiosity. But I thought, *it's none of your goddamn business*. Why? Because it didn't matter. It also wasn't my job to educate others about different kinds of lesbian parenting arrangements or appropriate terminology. What bothered me the most, was that I felt like identifying one of us as the biological mother would somehow mean more to the person who asked. The question about biological connection may have simply been about curiosity, but when it was asked, it reinforced my feelings of insecurity. I felt less adequate than Michelle. There were many things that we could both do in our parenting roles, like soothe him, feed him, or read to him, but being Finnley's biological parent was never something I could do or be.

When someone asked what Finnley was going to call us, it made me question my parental status, because it insinuated that there was only room for one "mom" in a couple – as if having two moms was unthinkable. I knew that's probably not what my friends meant, but that's how I felt. If I wasn't that *one* mom, who was I? The question about which one of us was the mom reminded me of my choice to be the non-biological parent. I had feared that my genes were not worth passing on because of my family's history of mental illness. I had to admit that those genes were also a part of *me* too.

If my son called me *and* Michelle Mom, I wondered if it would be confusing? Were we going to delay some sort of categorization part of his brain? Were we giving him some sort of non-binary complex? I logically knew that the answers to these questions were *No*. But when the closest people in my life brought up the topic, it did give me pause. I tried to push the doubts away, and not let them turn into something larger. I simply had to hang onto what I believed and knew to be true. That my son had two moms, and that was okay.

One of my neighbors and I had established a routine of saying *hello* when getting the mail or working in our gardens. The neighbor frequently waved to Finnley or stopped to remark how big he was getting. She was nice, but I didn't know her well. One day she asked, "Did you recently host a party?" I thought back in my memory bank, trying to recall if we had had guests over.

I said, "Oh yeah. We hosted a parenting group."

"There seemed to be a lot of women and babies," she responded, trailing off at the end of her sentence, almost implying the remark to be a question. She then asked if the women were *with* other women too, like me. I could tell she was trying to ask if they were gay, but didn't quite know how to say it.

I felt like I had to break the tension. I called out what she was too afraid or embarrassed to say. "Yes, we hosted our queer parenting group. Those were all couples and their babies."

She then asked, "How did *your* son come to be?"

Come to be? I thought. What does that mean? *How was he conceived? Where is his 'dad'? Did we use a turkey baster? What details was she asking for?* My mind quickly analyzed the situation again, determining just how much to divulge. I don't remember exactly how I responded, but I do remember the awkward pause that followed.

An eighty-year-old acquaintance of mine once referred to Michelle as "Dad." I simply said, "Actually, Finnley has two *moms*." I wasn't offended given her age, and she later came to me to apologize. She had never met a child with two moms before, but had the curiosity to respectfully inquire about what language we preferred. The more times I received this line of questioning, the more prepared I became. I could better decide on the fly whom I told what. I even created stock answers that I could repeat without hesitation. I liked to think that they politely told the person, it's none of your business. Or at the very least, got them to acknowledge to me and to themselves, what they were *really* asking.

"Who is Finnley's mom?"

"Finnley has two mothers."

The owner of Finnley's daycare made me feel the most uncomfortable.

She once asked me, "What's your name?"

"What?" I responded, thinking that I had misheard her. After taking my son to her establishment for the past six months, she should have clearly known my first name. I had a feeling I knew where this was going.

"What's your name, eh, what does Michelle, eh Finnley call you?"

I said, "Well, most people call me by my first name. Lora. Finnley has two moms, so each of us are called mom too."

I didn't need to know what Finnley was going to call us. Maybe he would call me *Mommy*. Maybe he would call Michelle *Mom*. Maybe we would be *Mama Lora* and *Mama Michelle*. I figured that the most likely scenario was that he probably wouldn't be able to say either of our names for a while. I figured he would probably come up with something totally unique and pronounceable on his own – which turned out to be true.

When Finnley was about two, "Lora" came out as "Yoda." It wasn't long before Michelle and Finnley started calling me "Mama Yoda." At first, I hated it. I didn't even like the movie *Star Wars*. All I could think about was that tiny, green, wrinkly, old-looking monster. I didn't want to be Yoda, I wanted to be Mom. But little by little, I started embracing it. It happened when I would come home, or pick Finnley up from daycare – he would light up when he saw me and say in a little toddler voice, "Mama Yoda!" It began to melt my heart. It made me feel special. How many other Mama Yodas did I know? Zero. The name was just for me.

Before long, my father-in-law gave me a Yoda doll for Christmas and a mug that had written on its front, *Yoda Best Mom Ever*. Michelle also started calling me Yoda on occasion. And there were variations too – Yo-ta and Yo-di. I was a newly appointed, all-knowing Jedi Grand Master!

When Finnley had a difficult time saying "Michelle" we brought back a nickname from her own childhood past. Michelle became "Mama Mimi." When Finnley's new childcare staff asked what he called us, I proudly said Mama Mimi and Mama Yoda, but it had taken me several months, possibly even a whole year, to gain that confidence.

Eventually, I wanted to own that word *Mom* outright. I wanted to feel totally comfortable with its use. But maybe it didn't totally fit because it's typically used to designate roles in a heterosexual relationship. Maybe it didn't quite fit because I was still figuring out what I wanted that word to mean. Maybe the word *Mom* was complicated because of the relationship I had with my own mother.

During the first year of Finnley's life, I navigated how and when to come out as his non-bio parent. There were times when it felt most appropriate not to reveal every detail – a nosy neighbor or work acquaintance does not need to know where my son's red hair "comes from." But in other situations, such as when my son was sick, I made my parental role explicit. This was the case because it related to his safety and well-being.

When Finnley was ten months old, we fed him a tiny mouthful of vegan chocolate pudding. It was delicious, so why not give him a tiny treat? Almost instantly he started having an allergic reaction. He threw up. He wailed. Large blotchy hives spread across his body, like islands on a map. This had never happened before. *What is going on?!* I thought. I looked over and read the pudding ingredients.

Chocolate, sugar, vanilla. Cashews.

A cashew is a nut.

Shit.

We had never given him cashews before.

In about five minutes we were out the door and in the car. I sat in the backseat alongside Finnley. He began to throw up again, choking on his vomit. We were still moving, but I unbuckled him and held him in my arms. He continued to cry. I felt scared and helpless, but tried to hold myself together.

We arrived at the hospital, which was thankfully only a five-minute drive away. Michelle went to park the car and I carried Finnley through the sliding doors. I checked him in at the reception desk. I talked to the nurses on staff. They seemed concerned and looked him over. By this time, Michelle had joined us. They handed her a clipboard.

"Go sit in the waiting room and fill out the paperwork," they said.

Go to the waiting room? I thought. We turned around and I heard them call at my back, "We will call you when we're ready." I looked around the lobby. It was a room full of patiently waiting adults. *Couldn't they see I was carrying a sick baby who could die from an allergic reaction?*

We sat down in the uncomfortable hospital chairs. Michelle began to fill out the paperwork. I continued to hold our exhausted son. My concern increased with each passing minute. Eventually, we heard Finnley's name being called and a nurse showed us to a small exam room and then they left us alone there.

I took off Finnley's shirt. It was worse than I thought. The red blotches were growing continents on his sea of pale skin. I couldn't stand the feeling of helplessness. I wondered what the hospital staff thought of our family unit. *Did they know me and Michelle were married? Did they care? Were they judging us?* Michelle had filled out the paperwork. *Did they think I was simply Michelle's friend and not Finnley's mother?*

I took Finnley in my arms and carried my half-naked son to the nurse's station. If I needed to parade my baby around to get someone to notice, I would. I found a nurse and asked for the third time, "When are we going to see a doctor?"

He responded, "The doctor has fourteen other patients."

I lost it. He released the Mama Bear in me. I thought, *This nurse is going to see me and my sick baby.* In that moment, I disregarded my strong aversion to conflict.

I demanded, "Do we need to go to a different ER?" I was prepared to get back in the car and drive to someone who would listen. Someone who would see. The nurse said, "A doctor will be with you shortly."

My demand seemed to change his body posture and tone of voice. Although I was still upset and rolled my eyes, I believed that help would be sent soon. I let go of my idea to huff out of the hospital and find another one and returned to the small exam room.

A few minutes later, a doctor finally arrived. Finnley's airway was not compromised. He received a shot and an oral medication. Apparently, the staff had made their assessment of Finnley while we were waiting in the main hospital lobby. They had been preparing his treatment, but no one had told us. Not a single nurse or staff person. All they had to say was, "Your son is having an allergic reaction, but we are doing something about it."

After Finnley was discharged, we drove the short distance back to the house and put our drowsy, pale baby to bed. The incident had scared us both. We bought epinephrine shots and learned how to use them. We took our son to an allergy specialist. Diagnosis: allergic to nuts.

Hello, nut-free household!

Finnley was also later diagnosed with egg and sesame allergies. The restless nights and frequent projectile vomiting of his younger days now made more sense. Michelle had probably eaten his allergens and then passed some of them to him through her breastmilk. I continued to feel like parenting was full of surprises.

A couple weeks later, I received a bill from the insurance company. I called to ask a few questions. They asked me my son's date of birth, which I provided. Then they asked me for my name, which I gave.

"I'm sorry, but your name is not on any of the paperwork."

Are you fucking kidding me?

How could I not be on the paperwork from the hospital visit? I thought back.

Car ride. Hospital entrance. Clipboard.

Then it hit me. I had been holding Finnley. Michelle had filled out the paperwork. She was the primary insurance carrier. My name must not have been registered anywhere.

I explained the situation to the customer service representative. She saw that Michelle and Finnley shared the same last name. But mine was different. I told her I was at the hospital too, but my *wife* signed everything.

I outed myself as gay.

I outed myself as Finnley's other mother.

I pointed out that Finnley's middle name is my last name. After some back and forth, she surrendered. I got the answers to my billing questions. But the situation had gotten under my skin. After years of feeling like people were judging me, I needed to start letting go of my insecurities. I needed to claim my parental rights because they had an impact on my son's safety and well-being.

When I was a kid, my mother's behaviors made me feel as if our lives were on constant public display. It made me want to stay hidden, unnoticed.

In elementary school, my mother's constant tardiness often left me waiting in the office far after all the other kids had been picked up. I tried to avoid eye contact with the secretary who had become a de facto babysitter. It felt like she was judging me and my family. I started to create an idea of what *normal* was. The kids who were picked up on time by their parents were normal, I was not.

While waiting one day after school was let out, my hunger got the best of me. I ate the holiday cookie ornament I had made in class, meant to hang on a Christmas tree. It felt like the secretary watched and disapproved of the eating. My five-year-old self, felt guilt about the cookie, and embarrassment for knowing that my mother wasn't like all the rest.

One afternoon when I was about six, I arrived home from school with my mother. We walked toward the front door, and she suddenly lost it. She was fuming mad, screaming at the neighborhood children who were playing in the cul-de-sac with their babysitter. I had played with those kids a hundred times. We had been friends. I couldn't figure out why she was so angry. I just knew that adults were not supposed to scream like that, especially at children. I sat on the threshold and hid in between the wooden front door and the metal screen door until the screaming was over. I never played with those kids again.

As an adult, I had to make a choice. Stay hidden in between the doors, or come out. Come out as gay. Come out as the non-bio mom, the second parent. I had to see beyond people's judgement and let go of the idea that I was less than. I realized that I had been carrying so much shame – that I wasn't a good person, that I wasn't a good enough parent. That shame had primarily come from my childhood experiences. From a young age, I had felt that others' eyes were watching me and judging me. This led me to believe I was different or not normal.

In addition, social norms reinforced my shame by frequently portraying a family as having one mom and one dad. I mostly saw examples of families with straight couples. Growing up, I wasn't exposed to *queerness*. I didn't know anyone until high school who identified as gay. And I certainly didn't know any queer parents with kids.

One of my first exposures to the idea of sexual orientation, was when I was about nine. My father used to eat dinner once per month with a male friend. My mother became jealous of their relationship and screamed that my father must be a *homosexual*! At the time, I only had a faint sense of what that word meant. I was too frightened to ask questions so the word just lingered in the air and inside my body.

As a child, it was difficult to trust my own feelings and perception of myself, because my reality was not validated by my parents. I saw one thing, but was told another. For most of my life, my mother believed that she had a rare and debilitating disease. When in reality, my mother's mental and physical ailments were likely due to her own childhood trauma and bipolar disorder.

When I questioned my father about this as an adult, he said that my mother had made appointments for tests, but had never actually followed through on taking them. He described a tumultuous trip to the Mayo Clinic in Arizona. My mother had a manic episode in the hotel, insisting that she had the disease, but never made it to the actual clinic for a diagnosis.

When my mother insisted that me and my sister had the disease too, we took a family trip to California when I was eight. My confusion and fear about why we had we were actually on the trip, resulted in me having a limp for the duration of our "vacation." I spent a day at Disneyland going on rides, but because my leg hurt so much, I got from place to place in one of the park's free wheelchairs.

After Disneyland, my sister and I were carted to a clinic where we were poked with needles and had our blood drawn. The test results were negative, yet my mother continued to tell us we had the disease forevermore. Feeling fine, I had to work hard to separate what I felt – from my mother's own beliefs.

Surrounding myself with other lesbian, non-bio moms made me feel more "normal." Learning about second parent adoption helped reduce my fear of the unknowns. And working with therapists specializing in trauma, helped me take back my sense of self. I learned to take pride in knowing I am okay the way that I am. I tried to see the times when I was a *good* parent. And I tried to embrace that word *mother*. I tried to separate old definitions from new ones.

With time, I learned to own being a lesbian, non-bio mom. I learned to own that term, *second parent*. I would do whatever it took to keep my family healthy and safe.

15

SECOND PARENT

Finnley was born into a politically tumultuous year, to put it lightly. In the fall of 2016, Donald Trump was running for president. Along with many, I was worried. Worried whether the status of my health insurance would be affected. Worried about the legal status of my marriage. But most of all, I worried whether the relationship with my newly born son would be legally recognized. Between tears and bouts of anger, I asked, *What does this election mean?* How will I be affected? There seemed to be so much hate coming from Trump on the radio and TV. He wanted to kick people out of the country, build a wall, take money from the poor, and strip LGBTQ rights away.

On election night, I tried to stay up to hear the final results. Finnley was only six weeks old and I was exhausted from lack of sleep. In the early hours of the evening, it seemed like Hillary Clinton would become our next president. But as the hours ticked by and more votes were tallied, my heart started to sink. I couldn't stay up any longer and headed to bed. I remember waking up in a haze to Michelle's voice, "Trump has won." I felt devastated, crawled back under the covers, and fell back to sleep.

On January 21, 2017, I walked several miles in the Seattle Womxn's March alongside 100,000 people. Trump's election was a historical and sharp pivot from Barrack Obama's presidency. Many of us in the queer community were scared and angry. In Queer Group, we talked about how our parenting rights might be affected.

That spring, the facilitator brought in a lawyer to speak. One of her specialties was working with people interested in doing second parent adoptions. This was the first time I had heard the term second parent adoption. It implied there was a "first" parent. I guess I had missed that episode of the L-Word. The one I later watched, where the main character, Bette, has to make the case that she is indeed a parent to a jaded social worker.

A second parent adoption (also called a "co-parent adoption") is a legal procedure that allows a same-sex parent, regardless of whether they're married to a partner, to adopt their partner's biological or adoptive child without terminating the "first" parent's legal rights.

I thought my rights as a parent were already safe because Michelle and I had legally married. We married in 2015, during a year of hope, when the Supreme Court ruled same-sex marriage legal in all fifty states. Here was a bona fide lawyer, saying that my rights as a parent were in question.

I said, "But what about our son's birth certificate?"

In the state of Washington, I could be, and was listed as Finnley's parent. She said that the legal lines were still murky. She implied that if something were to happen to Michelle, then someone else other than me could be deemed Finnley's legal guardian. I set out to do some research and learned what I could. I contacted a few other lawyers and attended a free class about second parent adoption.

After sifting through all the information, I believed my rights would likely be validated where I lived – "the gay friendly Northwest." If Finnley got sick and we had to go to the hospital, I believed we would deal with staff educated (and liberal) enough to validate my parental rights. If Michelle and I ever got a divorce, I believed a judge serving in Washington would legally grant me half custody.

But questions and unknowns still loomed. What if we traveled to a conservative pocket of the state? What if we crossed state borders? What if we traveled abroad? Would those people looking at flight tickets and passports, medical records, and legal documents, still allow me to make important decisions about Finnley's health or well-being? I wasn't willing to risk the answer being "*No*." This was my child. I wanted legal protections. I decided to seek second parent adoption and had Michelle's full support. I thought adoption would give me another layer of security, until the federal and state legal systems had fully sorted it out. Which I later learned, they may never do.

I wanted to do a second parent adoption because I have a fairly low risk tolerance. My fear of the unknown, makes me want to minimize the what ifs as much as possible. If there is something I can *do*, I usually do it.

When I was a kid, we flew out of an airport at least a few times for family vacation. But the trips always began on an anxious note. They began with my dad having us leave in the family car six hours before the flight took off. His reasoning was that if we got a flat tire, we needed enough time to fix it and still make our flight. He was a planner. He feared the unknowns. I had absorbed these types of behaviors over the years, not just from my mom but my dad too. And this wasn't just a one way trip I had begun, I was on a lifetime journey to protect my son. Everything wouldn't be in my control, but doing second parent adoption seemed like a good way for me to create a more stable future for my kid.

Once I decided to seek adoption, the question was how to start the process. No one was paying me for researching and trying to figure out how to navigate a complex legal system. Because I was working part-time, I had just enough "free" time to figure out who to eventually contact and what steps came next. However, had I been even more time-constrained, it would have been that much harder to find the time, energy, and money to seek second parent adoption.

When deciding whether to seek second parent adoption, one has to consider time off work, missed opportunities, or time away from family. There is also the toll it can take on emotional well-being which is hard to quantify, but important to consider.

At the free class hosted by the lawyers, I learned that I could file the paperwork myself. This would save on the costs of hiring a lawyer. But it soon became clear that the process was complicated. I would have to file the paperwork at the right time, pay the correct fees, and gather the right documents. When I initially started the second parent adoption process, I did so in a haze. At the time, Finnley was only five months old. He still wasn't sleeping through the night. He was bringing home every cold and sickness imaginable from daycare, which he started attending when he was three months old. Michelle and I were still figuring out our new roles as a couple, and as parents.

We didn't have thousands of dollars to spend on an expensive lawyer who specialized in second parent adoption. Michelle's employer had a program that would give $5,000 to an employee and his or her spouse who sought adoption. But after many emails and phone calls with "Corporate," the little we could understand from their response, was that the program was intended for parents adopting children through adoption agencies. Someone clarified that the program would not cover step parent adoptions. It remained unclear whether the program would cover second parent adoptions. We could try to use the program, but there was no guarantee they would reimburse the receipts.

Maybe getting reimbursed didn't seem like a good financial move. Instead, we turned to a legal plan that Michelle had signed our family up for, thinking we would use it to prepare a family will. I called the few lawyers from the plan who listed adoption as a focus area. But after contacting several, none of them seemed to know anything about second parent adoption or were willing to take my case.

Finally, I met with a lawyer who said she had worked with gay couples seeking to adopt who was listed on the legal plan. But her firm then assigned a junior lawyer to me instead. This lawyer was far greener in gay rights and second parent adoption. Nevertheless I stuck with her, since at least the majority of the lawyer's time would be paid for. I would have to cover all filing fees, printed materials (and, it turned out, the lawyer's parking fee at the county courthouse), but I had faith that she would submit the documents on time and help me through this legal ordeal.

Next, I learned that one of the primary steps to any adoption, is a social worker visit. Typically, a social worker inspects the house, pokes around, and asks intimate questions. This struck me as deeply invasive. These visits were typically intended for parents who had never met the kid before, but I had been Finnley's mom for months. Fortunately, some of my queer friends told me about a social worker who, in lieu of an at-home inspection, met with potential adoptive parents in her office. Even though the visit was less intrusive, I was nervous while she asked me many intimate questions about my relationship with my wife and my financials.

I was worried that she was going to ask about my childhood or upbringing, but she didn't. I sat in the social worker's office for one hour. The visit cost me $500, which is no small sum. The social worker fee could have been even more if she had traveled to my house to conduct the interview.

Like all other prospective adoptive parents, I also had to provide a set of documents that would accompany my court filing. And I had to have a physical examination with a medical doctor, I assumed, to verify my mental and physical competency.

When two straight people have a child, no one asks them to step on a scale or prove their mental capacity – they just go for it. So why was I expected to see a doctor to prove I could be – and was – a good parent? I didn't know what to expect because I had no idea what to ask for – or what the doctor could be looking for.

I changed out of my street clothes and into the lightweight medical gown. I felt exposed and vulnerable, as my naked legs dangled off the end of the exam room table. The doctor briefly looked at my chart and then perplexed, asked what I was doing there. I searched for the right words, but they didn't come out. "I'm trying to adopt my son, and I need to do a physical exam," is all I could say. The doctor gave a silent nod, then placed her cold stethoscope on my chest, looked in my ears, and examined my throat.

The exam only lasted ten minutes, but I couldn't shake how the experience left me feeling uncomfortable. I felt like I had given my power to someone else. Someone who in one stroke of a pen could say I was not parent material.

I had to submit paperwork to Finnley's pediatrician for his approval. Again, I tried to find the right words to accompany my request. I had visited this office so many times before. After months of taking Finnley to appointments and checkups, "I'm adopting my son" didn't feel right. But I tried my best to get the message across. I remembered that Finnley's doctor regularly wore a rainbow button on his name tag. I had high hopes he would understand. I was a good caretaker.

Lastly, I had to divulge my financial assets, listing where I worked, how much money I made, and the same for my wife. I had to make it clear to my lawyer that I wanted the documents to say, "second parent adoption" not "step parent adoption." I wasn't a step parent. My son was not the product of a split relationship, but the creation of a joint vision.

I logically understood that the adoption screening process was set up to protect children. It was set up so children would not enter unsafe homes, or fall into the hands of unfit parents. Still, those experiences were degrading. I thought, *I'm already Finnley's mother, why do I have to jump through these hoops?"*

After all the paperwork had finally been submitted, I got a court date. Michelle, Finnley, and I drove across the 520 bridge and headed toward Seattle. We parked the car, a few blocks away from the county courthouse. The entrance had metal detectors. *Not the most welcoming ambiance*, I thought.

Upstairs, we sat on a hard, wooden bench while waiting for a lawyer I had never met in person. All our communication had been done electronically. As my palms sweat, I imagined her holding a small piece of my fate. A person I did not know but had to trust.

A well-dressed woman approached us and introduced herself as my lawyer. She looked younger than me. In a flash, I wondered if she had kids. I wondered if she knew what it meant to identify with the word *parent*. I had faith that the rest of the adoption process would go smoothly, but there was still a part of me that imagined it crashing at my feet. *What if there was an error on the paperwork? What if I saw a judge who happened to be having a bad day?*

I didn't know what would come next. I tried to follow my lawyer's lead. I let her do the talking. We entered the small courtroom and everyone else cleared out, as adoption proceedings are closed to the public. An older gentleman of about sixty walked to the bench. He wore an official black robe. He was curt. Ready for business.

The hearing lasted only ten minutes. My lawyer briefly made her case. A few questions were asked. Then we were done.

For all the effort it had taken me to get to that court room, the social worker visit, medical exam, and documentation of finances, I thought the court meeting would have lasted longer. The court reporter suggested we take a picture. I guess I was supposed to be happy. Mostly, I felt relieved that the process was over. We walked behind the bench. It felt odd to be on the opposite side of where I had just been standing. Like I wasn't supposed to be there. As I stood with my family, I wondered why I had to be there at all. I wished that the process would have been easier. I wished that lesbian, non-bio moms like me, later down the road didn't have to do second parent adoptions at all.

Snap. The camera phone flashed. I was officially and legally considered Finnley's mother. I had just adopted my son.

We left the room, then rode the elevator back down to the lobby. I made chit-chat with my lawyer. She made a joke about being glad she could help. She usually participated in nasty divorces. My mind leaped to all the kids who got caught up in their parent's adult lives. I bet seeing their faces could take its toll.

We made our way back to the car. After months of checking off boxes, gathering documents, and going to the courthouse, I was glad to be done with it all. On the sidewalk, I picked up my son and held him high. I held on tight, feeling the pride that comes from being a parent. Feeling the love and joy that comes from being a mother. He was legally my son. I was legally his mother. Our relationship was protected.

16

LEGALITIES

Second parent adoption is the single most important legal procedure, if you are in a same-sex relationship, do not have a genetic connection to your child or did not give birth, and want to secure your parental rights.

As we drove away from the courthouse, the day of the adoption approval, I felt glad it was over. I didn't want to think about it anymore. I didn't want to be a second parent. I just wanted to be Finnley's mom. And I thought that I wouldn't revisit the topic of second parent adoption again. I was wrong.

Thankfully, I've never had to present my adoption papers to anyone to prove that I am Finnley's parent. However, when Finnley was about one year old, I had the time and energy to explore my second parent status a bit more. The conservative political climate only motivated me further.

I felt so hopeful back in June 2015, when the *White House* had been lit by rainbow colored flood lights. Facebook posts and photos of celebration and victory. The Supreme Court had made it known that denying same-sex marriage was unconstitutional (Obergefell v. Hodges). Shouldn't gay couples that marry get all the benefits that accompany straight couples who marry?

Marriages are doled out by the states, not the federal government. When you go to a county courthouse to get your marriage license, you're submitting it to the state where you reside. There is no national marriage license, or national marriage registry. This means your marriage is federally recognized, but the accompanying rights of that marriage, such as parentage, are determined by the state.

The truth is, states still hold a lot of legal power. I thought back to a commercial I had recently seen on TV from an organization called BeyondIdo.org. It featured a lesbian couple who had married: one of the women was a long-time teacher, but was fired from her job because she was gay.

Another commercial featured lesbian parents whose child was denied access by a pediatrician. Sexual orientation and gender identity are not protected classes in many states. The implications reach beyond parental rights. In 2016, only 19 states plus Washington DC protected against discrimination in housing, employment, and public spaces based on a person's sexual orientation and gender identity.

In 2018, the Supreme Court ruled in favor of a Colorado baker that did not want to make a cake for a gay couple's wedding (Masterpiece Cakeshop v. Colorado Civil Rights Commission). It is unclear how this ruling will affect similar cases in other states. What is clear, is that gay rights are still not fully protected in this country. With more conservative judges being appointed to long-term or life-time positions, it may be well into the future until every state gets on the same page regarding LGBTQ equality – and that may never happen.

The result of these systems has been a patchwork of state rights related to parentage, especially for the LGBTQ community. In one state, parental rights may be recognized because of marital status or issued birth certificates, but in another, those same rights may go unrecognized or be denied all together.

In Washington state where I lived, the fact that I was married before my son was born, and I was listed as his parent on the birth certificate, most likely meant that I would legally be considered a parent if Michelle and I ever broke up and she tried to take custody. However, a recent legal case casts some doubt on this. Brooke Barone fought for four years to be legally recognized as a parent in the eyes of New York State (Barone v. Chapman).

Barone and Chapman were long time partners, but unmarried during the time of their child's conception, and Barone never adopted the child. However, Barone played an active role in the child's life, even after Barone and Chapman split up. A lower court originally sided with Chapman, who wanted to deny Barone visitation rights, but a New York appeals court later overruled this in 2016. This case has the potential to set precedent for other non-married, non-bio parents seeking custody. However, this ruling does not affect a non-bio parent's legal status, while still in a relationship with their same-sex partner. In order to be able to make decisions about a child's welfare, it's still recommended by many for a non-bio parent to adopt his or her child.

In Tennessee, prior to federally recognized same-sex marriage, a husband from a straight married couple using donor sperm to get pregnant was legally presumed to be the "father," even though he did not have any genetic connection to the child. Because of this precedent, a lesbian non-bio mom like me would also need to be recognized as a parent. This led to the state seeking to deny parental rights for same-sex couples. In May 2017, HB 1111 was signed into law by Tennessee Governor, Haslam. The bill's goal was to define the words "husband, wife, mother and father." As a result, a parent in a same-sex relationship who was not the birth mother, could not be named the "mother" or "father."

Shortly thereafter, four same-sex couples brought a suit against the state of Tennessee. A judge dismissed the lawsuit, saying that the couples could not prove that their rights had been violated. However, accompanying the decision was an order stating that the couples were entitled to the same rights and protection as heterosexual couples whose children had been born through artificial insemination.

In 2017, the U.S. Supreme Court also ruled in favor of three married same-sex couples in Arkansas (Smith v Pavan). Prior to the ruling, the state would not issue birth certificates with both spouses names. Only the birth mother's name was allowed on the certificate. The Supreme Court ruled that both spouses names could be listed. Forebodingly, among the three judges dissenting in this ruling, was the recently appointed Neil Gorsuch.

With many of the Supreme Court judges getting older, it's only a matter of time before they retire or move on from their positions. This means that more conservative judges could be appointed who may rule in favor of denying LGBTQ rights. These future appointments have serious implications for queer, non-bio parents and same-sex couples. Even though our society appears to be getting more liberal in many ways, there continues to be a conservative base that is intentionally undermining LGBTQ rights.

This is where second parent adoption comes in. Adoptions granted in one state must be recognized in all the others. Regardless of where you adopted your child, if you move, your parental rights must still be legally recognized. This is also true if you move abroad, because of the Hague Convention. The Hague Convention established international standards and practices for intercountry adoptions. The long list of Convention countries, from Albania to Zambia, includes the United States.

Unfortunately, because parentage is still a patchwork of definitions by each state, it can be confusing and unclear about whether a lesbian, non-bio mom needs to do a second parent adoption. A parent must examine their risk tolerance and weigh it against the emotional, financial and time constraints that doing a second parent adoption brings. Speaking to a lawyer in your state is a good first step. But the important thing is that no matter what a single state says regarding their own parental definitions, if someone travels outside that state, they may encounter a vastly different circumstance. In short, even if one state says that doing a second parent adoption is not necessary, the same may not ring true elsewhere.

What is clear, is that a lesbian, non-bio mom's rights are more likely to be questioned by our social and legal landscapes than a straight person's. If a straight couple who is married, decided to use donor sperm because the man was infertile, it's unlikely the man would have to adopt the child to secure parental rights. And socially, many would assume he was the biological father anyway.

Does our society value straight couples more than queer ones? Do we want to create a society that helps protect children who come from committed relationships, regardless of sexual orientation? Because the U.S. is so politically and socially divided, the answers to these questions remain unclear.

I was still glad I had done second parent adoption, but disappointed to realize we weren't as far along on the equality scale as I had hoped.

There was a system that non-biological and non-birth parents like me could use in some states, but it didn't feel like it fit our situations. It was a good *fix* to our current problem, but I still held out hope, that maybe, someday it would be different.

Maybe someday the second parent adoption process would be available and easy to do in all states. Maybe someday second parent adoption wouldn't be needed at all. Maybe someday our name on a birth certificate or act of marriage would be enough to *prove* our parental rights, just like it was for straight parents. Until then, second parent adoption it is.

17

REGRESSIONS

Raising a newborn was *hard*. When the baby puked smelly vomit onto my shirt, it wasn't cute. It was gross. When the baby's diaper leaked diarrhea for the third time in an hour, I let out a sigh and asked myself, *How is this my life?* I'd scroll through my Facebook feed, because the baby had fallen asleep, literally on top of me. I was trapped. I looked at the pictures and read the witty comments, but they just brought me down. *Why is everyone else's baby so damn happy and smiling all the time? Why don't the other parents complain?* When I was in this state of mind, I felt alone in the night's darkness. I thought, *How can I be the only one feeling frustrated?*

We parents and prospective parents must get real with ourselves and each other. Just because you're not seeing or hearing about the difficult parts of parenting, doesn't mean they're not happening. I take responsibility for contributing to this problem myself.

Did I post any pictures when my baby had acne? No.

There is a gap of photos of Finnley from age two months to four months in my social media accounts. I didn't even know baby acne was a *thing* until my son was born. Why? Because we tend to share the "pretty" things in our parenting lives. Smiling faces. Play dates. Fun at the park.

I didn't share these experiences because I feared other people's judgement. This was especially true when I had feelings of frustration or anger about being a parent. Anger is such a negative word in most circles. I didn't want to be judged, so I typically kept these feelings to myself. But bottling them up wasn't healthy for anyone either.

When Finnley was nine months old I became interested in "sleep training." This was a concept I had learned about from the two parenting groups. By this time, I had also joined several queer parenting groups on Facebook. The social media pages were a wealth of knowledge. People asked questions about all sorts of things: potty training, post-partum depression, sleep training. There was so much advice at my fingertips and I felt like I needed it. When we moved into a new rental house, the sleep patterns we had previously created flew out the window.

Finnley was back to getting up every two hours. I felt like I was going crazy from the interrupted sleep. I scrolled through the parenting pages online and decided this was my ticket to salvation, "sleep training." Others had sworn by it. They described how after only two or three nights of "training," their baby slept through the night. The truth was, I hadn't done any real research about baby sleep patterns. Normally I would have gone for the science-based information, but because I was so sleep deprived, I chose what was more easily available – one paragraph accounts of positive experiences and how many "likes" the post got.

After an especially sleepless week, I told Michelle I wanted to try sleep training with Finnley. For his daytime naps, we had been letting him cry for 5 to10 minutes at a stretch. Michelle and I were both comfortable with this approach, because it seemed like it was helping him develop some self-soothing skills. If he didn't go to sleep within that window, we always returned to his crib to provide some comforting pats or to pick him up.

I was determined to do this approach and more at night. I was exhausted, frustrated, and tired of putting him to sleep every night which took one to two hours. Michelle agreed that we could try something different. I put Finnley in his pajamas, set him in the crib, then walked out the door. Immediately, he began to cry.

After a few minutes, Michelle said, "Do you think I should go in there?"

I said, "No, let's give it a few more minutes."

I was desperate and determined. This sleep training just had to work.

After we hit the ten minute mark, Michelle again said more firmly, "I think we should go in there."

And again, I said, "Let's keep trying."

A few months earlier in our Straight Group, there were a couple dads who had assisted with their kid's sleep training. They described how their wives had a difficult time with it, but they could stick it out. I thought that maybe I could fill this role too. Maybe I could do something that Michelle couldn't, because I was not the birth mom.

Ten minutes turned into twenty. Out of frustration and determination, I did not relinquish. I dug my heels in deeper. Michelle became irate.

"I can't do this! I can't be here!" she said angrily. She walked out of our house and through the front door.

Fifteen more minutes passed and Finnley began to wail. But by this time, my confidence in this method was feeling shaky. With each of Finnley's cries, my heart began to ache more and more. My baby needed me. *Why was I not going to him?* I thought that being the non-biological mother was going to make me tougher or stronger than Michelle. But in the end, I just had poor judgement.

I went outside and found Michelle sitting in the car. I carefully opened the door and said we were done. I was done. She didn't say anything at all, just opened the house door and walked inside. I could tell she was furious. Michelle went to Finnley's room and scooped him up. She was eventually able to calm him down by breastfeeding. Over the next hour, each of us went to bed quietly. Michelle and I didn't speak until the next morning.

When I woke up, I felt shame. My deep-rooted feelings of inadequacy from my childhood reemerged. As the days went on, I thought, *What is wrong with me?* Why had I thought that was a good idea? Part of me feared that I lacked empathy. Part of me feared that I didn't have the *right* parenting skills. It seemed to come so easily to Michelle.

My mind went to my childhood and how I had grown up. I feared that because I wasn't shown what positive parenting looked like when I was a kid, that I was destined to fail as an adult. But when Michelle and I discussed it over the next few months, I realized that I had simply made a mistake. I had been driven by desperation and sleep exhaustion.

I regret very few things in my life, but letting my baby cry for 45 minutes, while he desperately tried to get my attention, is one of them. Eventually, my shame turned into guilt. I knew that there wasn't something wrong with me, but I had done something wrong. My baby and wife needed me and instead, I had chosen to be stubborn. What bothered me was that I had wanted to go to Finnley while he was crying, but I hadn't trusted my genuine thoughts or feelings.

This experience taught me that I needed to let go of outside influences like social media and parenting group advice, and instead, trust my instincts. Being a non-biological parent didn't make me more deaf to Finnley's cries. It tore at me, from the insides out. I wanted to weep. Upon reflection, during that night of attempted "sleep training," instead of keeping him behind a closed door, I had wanted to pick him up and hold his body close. *That is what I was going to do next time,* I thought.

As a mother, I had to dig deeper. I had to figure out better ways to cope with my stress and lack of sleep. Our baby had a difficult time going to sleep and staying asleep. It seemed more difficult than other babies, but it was still in the realm of age-appropriate behavior. I had to adjust myself, because I was the adult. Over the next few months, Michelle and I discussed strategies for how we could both get more sleep. We took turns putting Finnley to bed while the other went to bed early. Although I couldn't breastfeed Finnley directly, I began to bottle feed him using milk that Michelle had previously pumped.

Finnley continued to be a large baby who needed a lot of sustenance to sustain him. His nightly feedings went on for what seemed like forever. Finally, at 17 months old, Finnley slept through the night. To capture the momentous occasion, I took him to the backyard for a picture. He sat on the deck with a little garden shovel in his hand. While the sunlight lit up his bright red hair, he stuck out his tongue, and I snapped the shot. Success.

18

PANCAKE PARTY

For Finnley's first birthday, we threw him an egg-free pancake party. Some parents want to see their kid's hand smash through a large chocolate cake, but that wasn't really my style. For starters, that sounded messy. Secondly, that seemed like way too much sugar for a tiny, human body to process. And thirdly, I was practical. When is the best time to interact with a one-year-old? Usually in the morning. We would avoid a meltdown, have ample time for a midday nap, and no one would overdose on sweets.

Pancakes are delicious. They also happen to be a breakfast food which kids and adults both enjoy. We asked our friends to bring their favorite toppings. About ten families trickled into our house, one-by-one. Most of our friends had children. I knew that everyone wouldn't arrive right at 9 am – many of them being on "baby time." Baby time being the extra minutes (or hours) it can take to leave the house when you have a small child. I expected that our friends would arrive in staggered waves, which was fine by me. The atmosphere had an energetic buzz, but the high-pitched screams and flying toys were a little overwhelming.

When it seemed liked most people had arrived, we pulled out a candle and placed it on a single pancake. There was whipped cream and sprinkles, so we weren't completely depriving our child of fun. The candle was a large, yellow, number "1." It had been given to us by my friend Bobby. Although we had lost touch over the years after high school, we had reacquainted after I moved to the Seattle area because he lived there too. Bobby's son had celebrated his first birthday the previous year. Bobby had also given us the party decorations, which happened to be rainbow-themed. It felt perfect. Bright colored orbs hung from our ceiling, and greeted people through the window as they approached our house.

After we lit the candle, everyone began to sing "Happy Birthday." If you ask me, that is one of the most melancholy tunes for a joyous event I've ever heard. But nonetheless, we all sang it with smiles on our faces.

Finnley looked around, bewildered to have so many people staring at him. I knew he wouldn't remember the moment, but I was glad we had celebrated it. One-year birthday parties aren't just for the kid. They're for the parents too. Taking care of a newborn was an all-consuming task. We had survived the first 365 days of parenthood. It felt like a grand accomplishment.

We had gotten through so many colds, bouts of stomach flu, sleepless nights, and moments of frustration. We had also experienced many joyous firsts. Rolling over, sitting up, smiles, and crawling. I had also completed the second parent adoption process and learned to embrace my new parenting role with more confidence. At the beginning of our trip, we were three individuals struggling to figure out our roles. But at the end of a year, we had grown into a functioning family with a steady rhythm and pace.

When the *Happy Birthday* song came to an end, I looked at the flaming candle. I let it burn for a few more seconds, then blew it out. After he ate, I helped Finnley get down from his chair and placed him near the other children. They looked like a pile of puppies. New to their bodies. Untethered in their actions.

We had bought three bottles of champagne to celebrate the year-long journey. I thought mimosas would surely be nice for celebrating. My friend Bobby saw them in the fridge when he first arrived.

"Those won't all get drunk, bet you'll have extra."

What did he mean by that? I thought.

As the pancakes were eaten and the topping bowls emptied, I filled cup after cup of coffee. The nights and days apparently still felt long for a lot of us. The orange juice stayed cold in the fridge. The champagne bottles remained unopened. I guess our mimosa-drinking, brunch-filled days were behind us. Bobby was right. He and his wife had two sons of their own. I guess they had gone through this phase before.

I still had some doubts about my role as a mother and parent when Finnley found comfort in Michelle instead of me. I tried to remind myself of the valuable contributions I made to the child-parent relationship. I connected and bonded with my son in ways that were special to us. I sang silly songs in the bathtub to make Finnley giggle. I made animal noises while reading books. I let him climb on my back. I played chase around the house like it was nobody's business. I began to see that those things don't have anything to do with being a "first" or "second" parent. It was simply about being a parent.

Being a parent allowed me to experience the innocence and joy of childhood. I got to laugh. I got to play. I got to act silly. I crawled on the floor, barked like a dog, contorted my face, made wild gestures, and created castles out of cardboard boxes. In many ways, these were the experiences that I wished I had had when I was a kid, but didn't.

A friend of mine who is a father, once told me that having a young child is like being a constant entertainer. I didn't understand what he meant at the time, but now I do. After a bad night's sleep, or when I hadn't had my coffee yet, being a clown at 6 am was exhausting. But there were many other times when being a parent was fun. When Finnley smiled at me, I couldn't help but smile back. I thought, *I was a part of that. I helped bring uncontrolled joy to this tiny human's life.* He reminded me to love without constraint. Without hesitation. To love fully, the individuals of both my families. Not yesterday or tomorrow. But in the present moment, wholeheartedly.

I started to feel the most gratitude in the smallest moments. I cried when Finnley's first words were "Thank you," in broken toddler English. His innocence reminded me that there is hope for this world. When he fell and got right back up, there was resiliency. When he failed but kept trying, there was persistence to succeed.

I loved seeing Finnley discover new things. I got to see the world through his eyes, like when he bent down and grabbed a rock to examine it more closely, or when he reached up to touch a wet leaf, because the dew caught his eye. He reminded me to slow down. Let go. Savor each moment. To celebrate the winnings of my own private jackpot.

When the party was wrapped up and our guests had left, I remembered the first time Finnley ran to me when I picked him up from daycare. He toddled toward me, arms stretched wide open for a hug. He brought me to my knees. I wrapped him in a warm embrace. There was nothing more special than seeing that recognition in his eyes. In that moment, I didn't need a piece of paper or someone else's definition – he was my child and I was his parent.

19

IDENTITY SHIFT

B efore becoming a parent, I didn't like shopping. I loved wandering the aisles for veggies and fruit, but if it was outside the produce department, I'd gladly let someone else load the shopping basket. If I felt compelled to buy clothes, kitchen gadgets, or household items, I usually had something specific in mind. No shopping meant I didn't have a lot of material possessions. Other than grocery items, Michelle typically handled household purchases. Although she didn't like many material possessions in her life either, she did enjoy finding "the deals" as we liked to call them.

After Finnley was born, online shopping got a hold of me.

When Finnley was a few months old, I heard from a friend that there were tiny gadgets that could suck boogers from a baby's nose. I thought, *that is exactly what I need*. Finnley had just been sick with a cold. The gadget sounded perfect.

I scrolled through the items on Amazon, barely looking at prices. If this gadget could help my baby breathe, plus get me more sleep, I was going to buy it. I found what I was looking for. I clicked the purchase button and started counting down the two days until the package would arrive.

Soon, there were other baby items that sounded useful too. Baby bathtub, white noise machine, sleep sacks, more burp cloths, and more swaddling blankets. Before Finnley had been born, I usually bought things locally or used at a thrift store. It felt extravagant getting all these new things online and shipped to my house. I felt guilty, thinking of all the natural resources being used. But, I could purchase all of these things in an instant. It was so easy.

Before I knew it, I had gone from a rare-shopper to a frequent-purchaser. I seldom paused to think about whether I really needed these things. Instead, I focused on my sleep exhaustion, and desperation for making a situation better. But as more items piled up, I started to view it as clutter. When I felt restless, I'd try to organize things, but they seemed to spill out quickly again from the closet. I missed the days of having only a few material possessions in my life. I missed keeping my socks in a Home Depot bucket instead of a dresser.

What kept me online shopping was the time it saved. Time became my most precious resource. It was quicker to swipe up or down on my phone than it was to get myself and Finnley into the car and into a shopping mall. A trip to the store meant carrying Finnley in the front carrier and feeling the resulting pain in my lower back. And he didn't much enjoy being in the "pouch," as I came to call it either. Buying things online, meant that I could skip the hassle of a trip to the store, and spend more time with Finnley at home. At least physically, it was more comfortable for us both.

Online shopping also filled my urge to find solutions to problems. And it wasn't just the shopping. I drove more than I used to. I was gardening less. I hadn't ridden my bike in months. I had signed myself up for a ready-to-eat meal delivery service. How did all that happen?

I used to pride myself in practicing what I preached – living out my values. I had a passion for protecting our earth, for being a steward of the environment. I used words like *sustainable, organic,* and *natural.*

Before moving to the Seattle area, I had never lived more than a few miles from where I worked. But after Finnley was born, I car-commuted 40 miles each day, then drove more after I arrived at work. I used to walk to the grocery store or a friend's house. I had even given up my bright red Subaru to drive an SUV. An SUV?! I would have never imagined myself in a tan Toyota Highlander. We had been given the aging vehicle by Michelle's parents because they didn't need it anymore. My Subaru was even older. We figured we would sell the Sube before it needed major costly repairs. Being a lesbian and owning a Subaru is like an inside joke among the queer community, because so many of us drive them. I was disappointed I couldn't be a part of that anymore.

I wondered if people would judge me for driving a gas-guzzling machine. But when I looked around, it seemed like a lot of parents drove them. I had to admit, lifting my son into a higher perched car seat was way easier on my back. I thought,

Maybe those other parents were on to something. But was I really like *them*?

After having an infant, my bike sat untouched in the garage. If I wanted to go anywhere and Finnley had to come, I used my car. Those first few months, just pushing a stroller on a bumpy sidewalk seemed to jostle his head too much. I could have biked when solo, but I found myself wanting to rush back home to give Michelle a break. I found myself using the car to drive a quarter mile to the grocery store. I increasingly took the path of least resistance and felt my old self falling by the wayside. *Was this the parent I wanted to be?*

I used to explore nature. Run through the woods. Hike up mountains. I've seen pictures of parents taking their tiny babies camping, so I know it's *possible*. But really, how much fun are they having? I've heard a saying that has stuck with me, which goes something like this: twice as hard, half the fun. Meaning when you have a small child, you can do the same things you used to, but they can feel like a lot more work and are less enjoyable.

Despite the strain on my back, there were still many times when I put Finnley in the pouch and went on walks or even picked blackberries. I strolled through my neighborhood and ventured to parks. But no matter how many trees there were, I always felt the urbanness of it. I longed to be in the open – to see tall peaks or walk alongside a babbling river. But when Finnley ate every hour, spit up constantly, needed to nap often, and couldn't hold his head up, making the trek to a remote nature spot did not sound like an adventure I wanted to take.

Since I was 18, I'd always had a pair of Chaco sandals in my closet. I'd gone through a few pairs since then. In the middle of winter, I'd look at them fondly and look forward to summer. Those sandals represented my carefree days.

After my son was born, my ten-year old pair of Chacos finally gave out. I didn't bother replacing them. I wondered if I was ever going to wade through a river on a hot sunny day again. I wondered if becoming a parent had taken away my ability to spend time in nature. Did it take away my drive to get out and have fun? I thought, *maybe my Chaco-wearing days are finally over.*

When my son was born, I gained a new identity. Mom. Even before Michelle gave birth, I started to view myself differently. I was prepping to be a parent. I mentally prepared for what it would be like to take care of a child. My wife and I were not only married, but future parenting partners.

There were times when questioning, ignorant, or disapproving people made me feel like the *other* mother. Like when they pried about why I didn't choose to get pregnant, or asked if I was going to be next – meaning, the next to get pregnant.

Most people who didn't know me well, assumed I was the birth mother when they saw me with my infant son. As I have a slender frame, strangers would make remarks like, "Wow! Your body looks amazing!" It was awkward, and I never quite figured out what to say. I felt like an imposter. But when I tried to justify the situation or explain myself, it never came out right. Likely because I was attempting to have a conversation about an intimate topic with a stranger. Fortunately, this phase only lasted a few months. As Finnley grew older, people stopped remarking about my body. I wanted to be recognized as a mom, but I didn't like being confused for the birth mother in this way either.

There were also times when I wanted to distance myself from that Mom identity. As Finnley got older, I felt like people weren't recognizing other aspects of me that I thought were important. They could only see me as a mom. I could barely see the old aspects of myself either.

When I was in the initial stages of parenthood, it felt as if I wasn't just losing habits, but parts of myself. I hadn't stopped doing one or two things. I had stopped doing *many* things and replaced them with behaviors that felt contradictory to my previous identity. I had stopped buying used items. I had stopped going to breweries. I had stopped using my bike. It felt like the parent part of my identity was muscling at the other parts. My newborn's needs were so high, it seemed that this was the way it had to be.

During that first year of Finnley's life, I felt like that's how it was going to be forever. There was a part of me that knew it would eventually get easier, but mostly, I felt stuck in the moments which were difficult. Feeling like I was giving in, or sacrificing my ideals made those feelings worse.

Before I knew it, I had a membership to Costco. A day I never thought would come. I bought all sorts of things there. Giant sacks of rice. Sixteen sponges at a time. Cases of canned tomatoes. We even made the plunge and bought a TV, because we were spending so much time at home. It was the first time I had ever owned a TV in my adult life. Prior to that, I had barely watched TV or shows on my laptop. It seemed like a waste of time. But after Finnley entered our lives, I let him sleep on my chest for hours, while I watched countless episodes of the show, *Chopped*.

When Finnley finally started sleeping better at night, around eighteen months, I felt like a whole new person. We only had to get up once or twice per night, a vast improvement compared to the previous twelve months. More importantly, I had enough energy to do more of the things I used to do in my pre-parenting days. Life seemed manageable enough. I could take myself off auto-pilot parenting mode.

Slowly, I started introducing old activities and habits back into my life. Finnley didn't need me at home every night to put him in bed. Michelle was totally able, capable, and willing to help. I found energy to read books again. I organized a book club. I started cooking more meals at home. I found energy for creativity. I wrote chapters in this book which I hadn't touched in nearly a year.

We bought a baby backpack and started taking Finnley on hikes. We didn't climb mountains or trek through snow, but we took ourselves into nature. Our "hikes" lasted an hour. But in that brief time, I got to be surrounded by tall trees and rolling rivers. I felt the uneven crunch of soil and rocks beneath my feet. Nature reminded me to slow down. It showed me there are systems out of my control, which function just fine on their own. Seeing a fern growing on top of a Douglas Fir, helped me appreciate my family and my role within it.

Did I want more some days? Yes.

Did I miss doing some of the things I used to do? Absolutely.

But did I want to be the same person I was before? No. I didn't.

An old friend I hadn't seen in a while invited me to see a movie in Seattle. I wavered about whether to go or not. As a parent of a young child, most of my weekend nights were spent at home. Finnley went to sleep at 7 pm, so someone had to remain at the house. I knew we could hire a babysitter, but I wasn't quite ready to take that step. I also thought about the expense. With Finnley in daycare, we didn't have much disposable income.

But then I started to think about how much I might enjoy an evening out with friends. I thought, *It could be fun to meet a few new people*. I thought of the adult conversations I could have. I looked forward to eating at a new restaurant and having a drink or two. The idea of dinner and movie became more appealing. I asked Michelle to stay at home and watch Finnley. I texted my friend that I wanted to join her.

In my old life, I would have taken public transportation into the city. But instead, I hopped in the Prius and headed east over the 520 bridge.

As I was driving, I heard the ding of a text message. It was inconvenient, but I found a spot to pull over to check my phone. My friend wanted to meet somewhere else. Plans changed.

I was glad to be in my car, and not on the bus. I made some turns, looked up new directions, and headed to the location in Uptown. It was a Saturday night and traffic was heavy. I drove around the block a few times and luckily found a cheap parking spot.

I walked into the restaurant and was greeted with a hug and smile from my friend. I thought, *Alright, this is going to be good*.

I slid into the booth, but the bench was high, and the table was low. I have a long torso, so I towered over the shorter people sitting next to me. It was a little awkward, but I tried to slouch so we could talk from the same height level.

I was introduced to everyone and started to make small talk. My friend decided to see a different movie playing at an earlier time. She and her friends already ordered food by the time I sat down. I told myself, *No worries, I'll just order a beer*. But the waitress was nowhere to be seen.

I tried to engage with the people around the table. I asked a few questions and got some responses. But I received few questions back. My friend's date was young and talked a lot about herself. They proceeded to caress each other at the table. I felt fine with a little PDA, but they increased their level of touching. Something about it made me uncomfortable. It wasn't the act itself, but the exclusivity. The scene was not how I thought the night would go. I had hoped for engaging, two-sided conversations.

The waitress then brought everyone's food to the table. It looked delicious and I could feel the soft rumbles of hunger in my stomach. I asked if the restaurant served beer. The waitress responded by saying, "I'll be right back."

A few minutes later she dropped off a menu. Again, I tried to order, but she said, "I'll be right back."

Everyone finished their meals. The waitress returned to clear the plates. She looked at me and asked, "Can I get you anything else?"

Anything else? I thought. I hadn't eaten or drunken *anything*.

But I simply responded, "No thanks." We needed to catch the movie.

In the theatre lobby I was introduced to a few more people.

They seemed nice. I asked someone how their night was going. One guy told me how he felt connected to the movie's main character. But he didn't ask me anything in return. I got the sense we didn't have much in common.

We all watched the movie, then headed out. I thought, *If this was five years ago, I would be up for getting drinks.* I would have wanted a night on the town with these people I didn't know. But what I wanted, was to go home.

Being a parent was trying to balance the old and new. I thought I would miss the partying, bar-hopping, and hanging out in large groups. But mostly I didn't. I still enjoyed meeting new people, going to movies, and eating at restaurants. But I wanted those experiences to feel meaningful because they had become so infrequent.

20

PARENTING

I've heard that the term *parenting* is a relatively new concept. It grew out of the seventies. Prior to that, people typically grew up in large families or stayed geographically close to their relatives. A prospective parent might have grown up with younger siblings, cousins, and neighborhood kids. By the age of 13, they might have already changed a few diapers, entertained some toddlers, or even done some serious babysitting. When people started having smaller families and moving for jobs, things changed. The family skills that we had previously passed from one generation to the next got lost along the way.

We now must acquire those similar parenting skills using different means. We seek the advice of researchers and parenting "experts." We learn how to take care of our children by reading parenting books. We take parenting classes and join parenting groups. There is so much information on parenting, that sometimes it feels like if you learn enough, you can do parenting the *right* way.

But to me, the word *parenting* falls short. As is, I envision the term being a one-way street. We seek parenting knowledge, so we can enact it upon our child. A parent teaches their child how to act, communicate, sleep, play, eat, love, and even how to go to the bathroom. I long for a verb that more accurately describes the act of *becoming* a parent. How in our new role as parents, we too are receivers of information. How we too, learn, grow, and change.

After becoming a parent, I saw the world through different eyes – through the eyes of a mother. A parent. When it comes to parent-child dynamics, I'm more sensitive than I used to be. It's like I feel more. Commercials make me tear up. A mother trying to find her son. A mother whose daughter was in an accident. In those moments, it's like I extend small pieces of my own heart to the parents. I think, *that mom could have been me*. Her daughter could have been *my* child.

Listening to the news has gotten harder to hear. Sunken ships. Migrants marching. School shootings. I don't just hear a voice on the radio. I imagine the families torn apart by tragedy. The lost sons and daughters, and the bereaved parents.

It had been two years since I spent quality time with my sister. Amy and I made a plan. I would take the bus down to see her in rural Oregon. Michelle would stay at home with Finnley. His daycare was closed one of the days I'd be gone, but Michelle's mom offered to come down and help.

Amy and I would drive to the Oregon Coast. It was an area that I hadn't visited in years, but whose tidepools, beaches, and salty mist, I loved. Amy took care of the accommodations; renting a condo through her time-share.

With everything lined up, I packed my bags, hopped on a bus, and headed south. When I arrived at the train station, I texted her that I had arrived. She pulled up in her white SUV.

It had been at least a year since I had ridden in a car with Amy. There was a place for me to sit in the passenger seat, but the rest of the car was *full*. Receipts, notes, gum, magazines, food, clothes. She showed me all the snacks she had packed in anticipation for our trip. This was a new level of preparedness I hadn't see from her before – and it reminded me of my mother. When our eyes met, there was no, "How was your bus ride?" or "How are you?" Instead, she said, "Do you mind if we go to the hospital? I need to take a test. I might have an infection." It was Saturday. I was a little surprised, but said, "Of course."

Over the ten-minute drive, she talked constantly.

We passed a restaurant and she said, "You've been there right? They have the best food."

"That's where I used to work. That's where I used to eat my lunches. Mom used to come sometimes."

"Do you see that canal? I used to see ducklings swim in there. Have you seen them?"

"That building is terrible. One time I parked in there and almost backed into a post."

"That building over there, is where my friend had his eye surgery."

"Where should I park? Do you think it's okay to park up there?"

When we pulled into the hospital driveway, and parked, I asked her to move a pile of papers on the dash because they were about to fall on me. The clutter reminded me of the house we grew up in and I could feel my own distress creeping in. "Can I put these in the back?" I asked.

She snapped, "No! There is dog hair back there. Just give them to me!"

Something seemed different. Over the last decade my sister had trouble organizing her thoughts, but this was a new level. There were so few pauses. Her brain and voice were in constant motion. One thought hopped to the next. To the next. To the next.

I walked into the hospital with her. Up to this point, she hadn't actually told me what the test was for, just that she wanted to take one. This was typical behavior for her. Dropping some seemingly important piece of information into my lap, but never actually providing the details. It was like she had to keep it secret. Or, perhaps it was an unconscious attempt at getting attention.

I sat in the hospital chair for about 30 minutes after Amy walked through some closed doors. When she emerged and we walked out of the hospital together, I finally asked why she had taken a test. She said she might have a urinary tract infection. Many of my friends had had them before, so I didn't understand why she felt like it had to be a secret. After gaining the information, I didn't press any further because I feared it would make her upset.

A couple hours later, we made it to Amy's house in the country. On the car ride, she'd told me she and her husband had spent hours cleaning in preparation for my arrival.

I walked up the carport steps and entered her house. The last time I'd been in her home, it was cluttered. But this time, every inch of flat surface had something on it. There was a chair in the middle of the kitchen. A sheet covered boxes in the living room. There were ten bottles of spaghetti sauce on the floor. The stove was covered in food, plates, and handwritten notes.

Amy was not in the room. Her husband John had just stepped into the kitchen near where I was standing. John and Amy had been married for 15 years. They married when Amy was in her mid twenties. John introduced Amy to conservative Christianity. She had dabbled in various church groups before they met, but his conservative Christian family was next level. They were nice people. But their values were different than my own. They didn't believe in abortion, didn't drink alcohol, and voted republican. When there were questions about life, they looked to God for an answer.

Previously, my sister's circles were more democratic and open to diversity of opinions. When Amy was in her early twenties we had reconnected while I was finishing up high school. I would drive to her small log cabin. I'd go there to get away from my mother and out of our house. We would tromp through the forest with her dog or hunt for deals at the local thrift store. When I was a senior in high school, we even drove to LA together, to see Madonna perform a concert.

In Amy's late twenties she managed to get an associate's degree and worked full time. But over the years, I saw my sister's independence and energy fade away. By her late-thirties, Amy had stopped working all together. John had become the sole provider for their family and from what I could tell, took care of all the things that took focus and detail: paying bills on time, picking up the mail, and ensuring that their cars were in working order.

I looked at John, and softly said, "It's kind of intense in here." He responded, "I want you to know, she has been cleaning for days. This area is much better than it used to be."

There was an awkward silence.

Amy's car had been making a noise. She told him that she was worried and anxious about it. John offered to take the car to a garage. He would get it quickly inspected and hopefully we would be on our way shortly thereafter. Starting to feel Amy's anxiety rise and wanting some distance from that, I offered to go with John to keep him company. What I was hoping for, was a moment where the two of us could discuss Amy's mental health.

At the car shop, we learned that the car needed repair so we wouldn't be able to take it to the coast. On the drive back to their house, I finally broached the subject of my sister's compulsive behaviors and stress level. I asked John if he had noticed anything different about her. His response was to say, "Yes. I haven't been praying as much as I could." He didn't elaborate and I didn't ask any more questions. But I thought to myself, *She doesn't need more prayer, she needs medicine and a therapist.*

When we returned to the house, John told Amy that we wouldn't be able to take the car to the coast. Amy became furious. If we took a different vehicle, she would have to transfer her carefully packed items from one car to the other. Her thoughts went to the snow-dusted roads. *Will we be able to make it over the coastal mountain pass? What if the car breaks down? What if I accidently leave something important behind?*

She started to yell, "I knew this would happen!"

"I made this happen."

I didn't know what she was referring to. I wondered if she thought she was cursed. I wondered if she was suffering from depression.

"I just knew we wouldn't be able to go!"

She began to cry. She began to sob while my pulse quickened.

"I don't have anyone to travel with."

"I can only ever go to the coast with mom."

"I'm stuck!"

The high expectations she had been carrying for weeks, came crashing at her feet. She went to the car that needed repair and pounded her heavy fists on the hood.

I started to feel the panic rise within me – the same panic I used to feel when I was young. It started in my chest. My breaths shortened. The feeling made its way up my shoulders, then spread to my neck and hands. My palms began to sweat.

I fought the urge to go into the house, lace up my urban shoes, and run the five miles back into town. I could have run past the rolling hills and wet fields. Past the dirty donkeys standing in their mud-filled paddocks. Past the broken-down farm equipment. Past the ferns dampened by winter, whose brown fallen remains, still reminded me that spring hadn't yet come.

But instead, I stayed.

I saw my sister. I saw someone's child. I saw someone's daughter.

As a parent, I saw all the ways that my sister should have been better taken care of by our own parents. I imagined my mom trying to take care of Amy when she was young. I thought about my dad traveling for days and weeks at a time for work. I imagined how my mom's mental illness could not provide Amy the emotional tools that might have helped her. I felt as though I was straddling a line between two circles. One circle filled with the family I grew up with. The second circle filled by the new family which I had created.

My sister's actions reminded me of my son's. A child who felt deep and raw emotion, but didn't have the tools to deal with them. I saw how Amy possessed many of my same tendencies; a disdain for change and the desire for control, but how they had been amplified by tenfold.

While standing in my slippers, under the freezing carport, I asked my sister to give me a hug. At first, she refused. As she continued to cry, I felt tears welling in my own eyes. I quickly wiped them away as they rolled down my cheeks. I was determined to be the steady one. The even one. The person maintaining control.

Some habits linger far after you want to let them go.

Amy finally walked toward me. I embraced her tightly. She didn't hug me back, but I told her, "It's going to be okay. We don't have to go to the coast."

I could see that it was too much for her. I let her cry on my shoulder.

I was filled with grief over Amy's debilitating anxiety. I missed my sister – the person she used to be. Growing up with her had been difficult, but we were two sisters who had shared a history and a particular mother. I used to be able to talk to her. To have conversations. To go on fun trips. But so much had changed since we were kids.

I wanted to help her but I couldn't. She was not a child. We were two grown women, standing in the cold under a carport.

After Amy calmed down, I walked inside. Controlling my panic, I reached for my phone to look up bus schedules. Scroll. Scroll. Click. *Maybe I could get on a different bus, one day early, I told myself.* The pages slowly loaded. The browser wouldn't refresh. *Damn this dilapidated countryside,* I thought.

With the limited cell service I got, I discovered that I could still send a text message. I reached out to Michelle and briefly explained the situation with a few words. I hit Send. I put my phone down then headed to the shower.

I let the hot water hit my neck. I felt it roll down my shoulders. I told myself, *I am strong.* I reached down deep, searching for the tools I had fought hard to acquire over the years. I told myself to breathe – slow and long.

I got out of the shower, dried off, and returned to my phone. There was a voicemail from Michelle. She acknowledged the one word that had been echoing in my brain. She guessed how I must have felt: *trapped.* I let the word repeat in my mind, *trapped, trapped, trapped.*

I thought of the family that I had created. My wife and child. I closed my eyes, and saw their faces. The only place I wanted to be was home.

John didn't offer any advice or opinions, at least none that I could hear. I think he had learned to accept Amy as she was. He had accepted her behavior and treaded lightly to decrease conflict. I wanted him to fight for her health and well-being. Maybe he was, but I wanted him to do it differently. I wanted him to rely on more than just God's benevolence.

The next day, I guiltily asked my sister to drive me to a car rental agency. I knew my sister ached to connect. If I stayed another 26 hours, I could have gotten on a bus with a ticket I'd already purchased. The one I had planned to take. It was only one extra day. I could have stayed.

But I didn't.

The thought of the constant chatter and cluttered house were too much for me. The tools I carried could only take me so far during this trip. I wished that it was different, but it wasn't. I loved my sister. I wanted to accept her as she was, but I couldn't.

I got into the rental car and made the five-hour trip back north. I drove through Oregon, then Washington. Up I-5 then the 405. I exited off the freeway and dropped off the rental car. I began the mile-long walk to my house.

I wondered why some kids turn out the way they do. My sister and I came from the same family tree. We shared the same genetics. But it felt like our tree had split into two different branches. I imagined how genetics and upbringing mingle, mix, and mash, to create a whole person. How along the way, there are twists and turns. How in some instances a child is pushed down, and in others, they are given a helping hand. I was reminded how fragile life is. How there are no guarantees. Even when we try our best. Even when we seek the tools to change our understanding. Sometimes we are still left without answers.

I walked up the driveway and looked through the window. I spied Finnley inside and tapped on the window. I gave him a big smile, and he returned it. I went inside to my child sitting on the floor and held him tight. I felt his soft skin on my cheek. I let the chaos of my trip roll off my shoulders.

Then, from the corner of my eye, I spotted something out of place. Something different. Something new.

I looked at the area closer. My eyes caught sight of three giant boxes, one stacked atop the other. I let go of Finnley and walked toward them. I looked down at the brown wrapping. Each of the boxes was addressed from my mother.

I imagined the menagerie of mismatched items that awaited inside and went back to where Finnley was sitting on the ground in the living room. He looked up from a picture book. I returned his gaze and gave him a second hug, stronger than the first.

21

TRYING AGAIN

Raising a toddler was so different than caring for a newborn. Instead of the night bringing a challenge due to lack of sleep, it was the daytime that felt tiring. By 15 months, Finnley was in constant motion. He needed stimulation. He pushed boundaries. He wanted things, *now*. But a slight ease had entered our lives. There were enough restful periods in between the busyness that left me with just enough energy, that I thought, *maybe, just maybe, I could do this all over again.*

In an ideal world, where money and time didn't exist, Michelle and I thought we would have three children. We both liked the idea of building a little tribe. My friends who came from larger families seemed to genuinely like their siblings and were close to their parents too. The kids would always have someone to talk to, play with, or complain to. I knew I was romanticizing the idea, but still, it seemed like a picture I wanted to create.

Being practical about our energy levels and financial resources, we would realistically have two kids. Michelle got easily pregnant the first time around, but there would be so many unknowns about a future child. If we did IUI again, how long would it take? How much would it cost? Would I feel like the *second* parent all over again?

I imagined Finnley and his future brother or sister, playing in the back yard. Riding their bikes in front of our house. When they were in school, I would attend their basketball games or mathlete competitions. Michelle and I would both be working, but in the summers, we would carve out time to go on family vacations. There would be camping trips, adventures to the coast, and weekend hikes. I also imagined that the kids would steal each other's toys, squabble in the car, and not always get along. But still, I hoped they would enjoy each other's company as they got older. At the very least, they would both be able to share what it's like to have two moms.

When Finnley was a little over a year old, Michelle said she was ready to start trying for another child. I initially had some reservations. We were just finding that new family rhythm. It felt like life had just gotten easier. I wanted to get my bearings, at least for a couple more months. Michelle and I weren't quite on the same page. There was part of me that felt like something was wrong with me. *How could Michelle be ready, and not me? Who was she, Wonder Woman?* But Michelle had always been better at dealing with stress than me, so I shouldn't have been surprised that she was ready to grow our family sooner than I was.

After a few more conversations, Michelle agreed that we would wait a bit. She had only recently stopped breastfeeding and her periods still weren't regular anyway. We would wait two more months for everything to even out, then start trying. Besides, it was winter. The holidays were just around the corner. Not that we celebrated much, but we had several out-of-town trips already planned. They would give us time to do a little more planning – Michelle could track her periods. We could figure out just how much frozen sperm we had left, queue it up at the fertility clinic, and set up a few doctor appointments.

After Finnley was born, I thought I might feel differently about getting pregnant myself. I had expected that I would have gained clarity in the matter. But over a year had gone by, and I still didn't feel a definite urge either to get pregnant or a definite aversion to the idea. Being Finnley's mom had given me more confidence that not having a genetic connection was okay. Nothing about my family's history of mental illness had changed. If we were only going to have two children, this was my last opportunity to get pregnant if I wanted to.

Because I still had occasional bouts with insecurity, I found myself pointing out the times when it felt like Finnley loved Michelle more than me. I'd try to pass my comments off as a joke, but Michelle called me out. One evening, she snapped, "Why do you do this?"

Michelle accused me of being blind to all the times when Finnley chose me instead of her. I had to admit, sometimes it was easier for me to perceive negatives, than positives. And I realized that it could be destructive to make such comments in front of

Finnley. The older he got, the more language he would understand, spoken and unspoken. I didn't want to make him feel judged or self-conscious about his feelings and experiences.

So, I stopped with the comments. I genuinely tried to stop looking for the occasions when Finnley "chose" Michelle instead of me. Sometimes I still *thought* he wasn't choosing me. But not vocalizing those thoughts helped reduce my insecurities. I started to see those moments less frequently. It felt like one of those cheesy mantras – say something enough times, and you will start to believe it. *Not* to point out the moments became my silent mantra. An unconscious stream of connected thought started to form. It said, "I am not the other mother or second parent. I am a parent. I am a mom, just like my wife." And in small and large ways, those unspoken words rang true.

It was evening and Michelle and I were lying in bed. I reached over and was about to turn off the light of my nightstand. Finnley had recently been sleeping better, but in the last few days he had slept terrible again. He woke up at least three to five times per evening. My brain and body went back to the beginning when he was first born. Almost like muscle memory, my tiredness set in. I thought we were past this. *But who was I kidding?*

I wasn't sure what was going on. Maybe it was the pain of new teeth poking through, or that crummy cough brought by a recent cold. It could have been a thousand things, all of which I had zero control over. I reminded myself to let go. Let go. Let go.

From his room just down the hall, I heard Finnley begin to whimper. Michelle leaned over toward me and said, "Will you go check on him? I don't know what to do."

Admitting to *not* knowing something was uncharacteristic of my wife.

I asked, "What do you mean?"

She responded, "I go in there and pat his butt, but I don't feel like it does anything."

I was surprised to hear her say this. She went on, "You know how to soothe him better than me." *Really?* I thought.

I had spent so long focusing on my wife's mothering abilities that I hadn't left room to recognize my own. Michelle went on to say that her go-to of breastfeeding was no longer an option, since she'd ended that ritual the month before. Just about every time he previously cried, she had relied on that way of providing comfort. And it almost always worked – like a charm!

Just as I had to so many times before, she was navigating a new way to interact with her son. On the one hand, I felt a little sad for them both. They no longer had the thing that bonded them so tightly. But on the flip side, although our son still cried at night, he always eventually was able to settle down. He too was learning. He just needed some additional reassurance from his parents.

I looked at Michelle and we both smiled. I felt like I was doing a "mom thing" better than she was. She smiled because she was admitting it. I walked down the hall to Finnley's room and opened the door. It was dark, but I knew where to go, and what to do. I was a mom.

I felt the confidence I needed, to say yes to having a second child. I felt that Finnley was my child in every way other than genetically. I had struggled with my bouts of insecurity and fear, but with every month that passed, the fear I held about turning into my mother or not doing a good enough job started to dissipate.

Michelle and I discussed again whether I wanted to get pregnant – and the answer was, no. I still felt some sadness, knowing that I would never feel a baby kick inside my belly, but acknowledging those feelings helped me let go of them. Michelle said she was okay with getting pregnant again, so we agreed that was our path going forward.

Choosing to use the same donor sperm for our second child was also a conscious choice. Finnley had turned out to be the child we had hoped for. *Why not try again with the same donor sperm?* I knew the next pregnancy and next child would not be exactly the same. But the *trying* part had been relatively easy enough.

After the first round of IUI to create our second child, and during those first few days that followed, I asked Michelle, "Do you feel anything? Do you feel different?" There was a *maybe*, a twinge, an unexpected gurgle. "Could it be?" we asked.

Maybe, maybe, maybe.

But when it came time to pee on that stick, the result was negative. We were a little surprised after Michelle got pregnant so easily the first time, but we admitted that the odds would likely mean more tries were needed. Those tiny blue letters, in a tiny white box, "Not Pregnant," were a reminder that there are some limits which cannot be broken, no matter how much you want them to be.

After Michelle got pregnant with Finnley, we were able to

purchase a few more vials which eventually had come out of quarantine. After the first failed attempt at IUI, we only had three more vials of our donor sperm left. Would it be enough to result in our hopes turning into a reality?

After a trip to the fertility clinic, a second IUI, and a second negative pregnancy test, my hope started to diminish. We had already spent money on the sperm itself and for the sperm storage too.

Only two vials of sperm remained. Michelle messaged her contact at the fertility clinic via the online portal. It was easy enough to make contact online, but getting an actual appointment seemed impossible. We sought advice on how to make the most out of those two remaining vials. We thought that a brief consultation with a doctor could help. But the clinic was so busy, Michelle couldn't see anyone before her next cycle began.

Michelle devoted more time and energy to getting pregnant than she had done while trying to get pregnant with Finnley. There were days to count before and after a period. Hours to count after an LHL surge. Days to count after the IUI. Every time the pregnancy test read negative, the effort of tracking numbers, cycles, and missed opportunities had to be repeated. The process started to take a toll. Michelle was tired of tracking her period, not drinking alcohol, and feeling disappointed. I too was tired of waiting and feeling disappointed when the pregnancy tests were negative.

We couldn't get in to see a doctor on the schedule we wanted, but the fertility clinic contact reached out to Michelle and suggested two possible ways to increase the chances of Michelle getting pregnant. The first was a drug that would encourage

Michelle's body to release more than one follicle (immature egg) during ovulation. We scanned the long list of the drug details and warnings. The label noted that the chances of producing twins could be increased, but those odds were low. Michelle consumed a tiny white pill every morning for five consecutive days. When the last pill was gone, we made an appointment for an ultrasound.

The second suggestion to increase our chance of pregnancy was to use a "trigger injection" combined with an ultrasound. It sounded a little scary, but it was only a small needle. After examining the follicles on an ultrasound, the injection would be given in her belly. The fertility doctor said I could give Michelle the injection or she could do it herself. But needles freaked me out and Michelle was indifferent. After ordering the drug online, we figured we would head to the clinic and have the nurse do the injection, then twenty-four hours later, Michelle would have the IUI procedure done. The drug was all about timing. Instead of having a 12 to 48 hour window in which an LHL surge can occur, the drug narrowed that window to about 24 to 36 hours. Thus, we would be increasing Michelle's chance of getting pregnant by doing the insemination at just the right time.

But first, we needed to get our hands on that injection drug. It needed to be ordered from an out-of-state distributor. It also had to be kept cool, otherwise it would degrade. Michelle called the company's number. After several attempts at making contact, being on hold, and trying to call in between work meetings, she was able to place the order. The drug was in transit and set to arrive on Tuesday.

Tuesday arrived, but there was no package. Instead, when I

arrived home from running errands, there was a delivery tag stuck to our door. There was a handwritten, scribbled, mystery word on the tag. *Neighbor*, I thought? I walked to the neighbor's house and knocked on the door. When they didn't answer, I left them a voicemail.

Five minutes later, I looked out the window and saw my neighbor walking toward our house. When I extended my arms to take the brown package in his hand, I hoped he wouldn't ask what was inside. I didn't want to explain that we were trying to get my wife pregnant. We were on friendly terms, but I didn't have the energy to go there. If he asked, I would feign ignorance, stating that I didn't know what Michelle had ordered.

Luckily, when the package made its ways into my hands, no questions were asked. I said, "Thank you," and closed the door.

I opened the package, and much to my surprise, there was a note, attached to soft blue paper. It read, "Good luck on your journey to creating a family." I smiled, and pulled the handle on the fridge, placing the single shot on the flat shelf. It sat there quietly, as plain as could be next to the yogurt and leftover rice. Maybe this shot, plus the rest of our cocktail of chance, really could help us have a baby.

22

JUMP

Maintaining a committed relationship with Michelle took work. This was especially true after having a kid. Sometimes words left my lips faster than regret closed the door. Sometimes I wanted to sleep on the couch, and on the rare night, I did. Sometimes the day-to-day grind left me longing to experience something new.

Time was scarce – time to give myself or Michelle. I had to figure out ways to turn off Netflix, even though it beckoned me with the promise of late-night comfort. I had to look away from the allure of a bright-screened phone. Michelle and I needed some time together where we could emotionally connect.

It had been over two years since Michelle and I had spent more than a single night away together. We spent a lot of time together at home when Finnley was young, but many of our conversations were short and to the point.

"Did you change Finnley's diaper yet?"

"Yep."

"Can you pick Finnley up from daycare this afternoon?"

"Yes."

In between caring for our son, our home, and going to our jobs, it left little time for intimacy. The time we did share became so interrupted and scarce. When Finnley began to speak, we could hardly have more than a 30 second conversation before he had to weigh in on the matter.

When Michelle or I would leave the house to do things like go to work or pick up groceries, instead of saying "See you soon," we would say, "See you never." It became our inside joke. Instead of feeling frustrated about time interrupted, it lightened the situation and made each of us smile. In those small moments, we could see each other. It was like we were saying, "It's crazy busy right now, but it will get better soon."

Perhaps going on a vacation without our son could provide us some room to slow down, relax, and connect.

After having lived in Kirkland for three years, an area mostly comprised of office parks and highways, I wanted to be in nature. I wanted to walk on trails. Look up at the night's sky and see stars. These were some of the things Michelle and I used to do together, before Finnley entered our lives. Michelle and I agreed that it was time for our own adventure, even if it was only for a few days.

With several months' notice, we started to plan. We explored our travel options. We looked at places that were relatively easy to get to by plane, but wouldn't break the bank. Eventually we settled on flying into Las Vegas, and from there, we could go to Zion National Park and Bryce Canyon. These were two places that had been on both of our must-see-someday lists.

Michelle booked the tickets and rental car. I turned through pages of a *Lonely Planet* guide book. Over the course of a week, I managed to nab some campground spots online, that were previously all rented out. I imagined Michelle and I cuddling together inside a small tent. It looked like luck was on our side.

Halfway through the hatched idea and reservation process, we reached out to Michelle's parents. They were willing to drive down from Bellingham to help out.

Over the course of a year and a half, Michelle and I had repeatedly discussed the idea of looking for an in-town babysitter, that of the high school or college variety, but the need had not surpassed our lack of desire or financial resources.

Nana and Papa were great caretakers. I continually felt fortunate to have such loving, nurturing, and non-judgmental in-laws. They expressed interest in being active grandparents, but didn't smother us in gifts or advice.

After Nana and Papa arrived, Michelle and I drove to the SeaTac airport and made it through the long TSA line. We had an unremarkable flight, including boarding, taking off, and landing. We noticed how easy it was to travel without a baby. So what if there was a long line or turbulence? It didn't matter. We could take care of our own basic needs with ease. A novelty after almost two years of taking care of a tiny human.

When we arrived, we picked up the rental car then drove to Zion National Park. The views were beautiful. A lot of open space at first, then large red rocks popped up from the landscape. We found our campsite which was nestled in a small valley, surrounded by towering rocks.

On the second night of our trip to Utah, Michelle and I lay inside a hot tent. The day's light was dimming. I asked, "Are you going to take the test tomorrow, or the next day?"

A couple weeks prior, Michelle had completed her third round of IUI. I was asking when she was going to take the pregnancy test. She responded with some numbers and statistics, stating that the odds of us waiting one more day would provide a more accurate result. It was difficult for me, but I could see her logic in waiting a little longer.

My memory went back to a conversation we had almost six years prior. It was that time when our relationship was as green as the ponderosa pine needles. When we laid in a different tent while camping at that spot near Bend, Oregon. It was when Michelle said she wanted kids - and I sat with what that might mean for me.

In an instant, my mind replayed the discussions, experiences, and times we had spent together that equaled *here*. I thought about how it used to just be me. After spending four years in a city of roses, biking between houses, packing boxes, and creating a home, me had become we. After sharing silver rings and firelit conversations, we had turned into three. While lying under monolithic red cliffs, our family proclaimed more – a readiness to become four.

Thirty six hours passed. One whole day and one full night. Michelle pulled the pregnancy test from its box and slipped it into her jacket pocket. We made the short trek to the campground bathroom.

I pulled open the bathroom door. Michelle followed behind me. We were strategic. Only entering after all other occupants had vacated. We walked toward the back. Toward the largest stall that could contain both of us, and our excitement. There was something about this latest round of IUI. This small plastic test, sitting in Michelle's front jacket pocket. Something was different than the other previous two attempts.

I *knew* it. I *felt* it. Michelle was pregnant.

Michelle and I entered the campground bathroom stall. She carefully peed on the stick, then laid it down on top of the metal toilet paper dispenser. Again, I had a feeling that I knew what the result would show.

For starters, Michelle had been increasingly irritable over the last few days. Nothing major, but my annoying tendencies, like leaving my dirty socks on the floor or asking her to do something while she was already doing something, got under her skin. She would snap at me, "Don't talk to me like that."

Michelle pounced on the opportunity to point out my missteps. I made a mental note to be more accommodating and respectful of her needs. I also thought back to two years ago, feeling a sense of deja vu. That, on top of her increased tiredness seemed like clues which could not be ignored. I tried not to get my hopes up too much, but secretly, they grew larger.

Michelle and I looked at each other nervously, as the circle blinked inside the tiny white box. Thinking, thinking, thinking, it said. Three minutes of waiting.

Finally, it read "Positive."

I knew it! We turned to each other, giddy with excitement.

I wanted to capture this crazy, beautiful, surreal, moment of my life. I pulled out my phone, and took a picture of Michelle holding the pregnancy test. "Yayeee," she exclaimed, and smiled wildly.

Michelle threw the pregnancy test in the trash on our way out. We walked back to our campsite, packed up the tent, and loaded the car.

Driving onward to Bryce Canyon, something struck me. Not once in that campground bathroom, had I felt like something was missing. I didn't feel jealousy or insecurity. I didn't feel regret or fear of missing out. I didn't feel second or like the other mother.

Instead, I felt joy. Joy from hopes turned into a reality. I had traveled on my own path to parenthood and would soon be starting another. I didn't know how I would feel, or what it would be like. But by listening to my instincts, I knew it would be different.

So much had changed since Finnley was born.

My relationship as a parent-to-be had changed. Even the relationship with my own mother and sister was slowly turning into something new.

Michelle and I spent the rest of our vacation jumping. Seeing that positive pregnancy test meant that we were on our way to raising another child and growing our family.

I would identify a beautiful spot, then challenge Michelle to capture me in mid-air with the camera. We were on top of a canyon looking below. Michelle sprang up, and I clicked the camera

– focus aimed at her gravity defying body. I was on vacation with a wife that I loved. We had made so many jumps together over the years – into dumpsters filled with bagels, renovating a house, getting married, and starting our family. Somehow, we had always managed to land safely on the ground.

23

ONWARD

During week nine of Michelle's second pregnancy, I found myself in a dark room, looking up at a monitor screen. A nurse was probing Michelle's insides with a phallic looking medical wand. We would have normally skipped this ultrasound as an option, but Michelle and I were both feeling anxious about the possibility she might be pregnant with twins. The odds were incredibly low. But it had crossed our minds as a possibility. The trigger injection she had received before the last round of insemination had caused her body to release two follicles instead of one. If Michelle was carrying twins, our lives would get crazy. Like, *really* crazy. The thought of taking care of two infants (plus a toddler), seemed terrifying and exciting all at the same time. It would be a tremendous amount of work and money, but we could do it. The prospect of twins also stoked my unrealistic yearnings of someday having three children – that idea

Michelle and I had hatched before Finnley was conceived.

The nurse turned the wand toward the embryo's yolk sack. She plainly said, "The size and shape appear to be good." She turned the wand some more. My eyes went back and forth between Michelle and the black and white image on the monitor screen hanging overhead. The nurse paused.

"It appears you have twins," she said.

I felt a rush of adrenaline and squeezed Michelle's arm. But then the nurse quickly added, "I want you to emotionally prepare yourselves, that things might change."

Things might change. Things might change, Things might change, my mind repeated.

"What do you mean?" I asked.

"One of the yolk sacks is much smaller than the other," she responded.

My eyes darted to the screen again, trying to follow the red measurements she was drawing with the click of a computer mouse. I could not see what she was describing. Then there was the single image – both yolk sacks side-by-side.

"Oh wow," I said, unconsciously letting the words, softly spill out of my mouth.

The nurse quietly said, "Yes." As if she could tell that I finally understood what she meant. "Twin B" was remarkably smaller than "Twin A."

"Any medical professional could tell that there are differences here," she said.

My mind raced. *What exactly did that mean?* It did not sound good.

The nurse then described how sometimes, a less thriving twin can get reabsorbed by the mother, known medically, as a "vanishing twin."

Twin B was smaller and had a slower heartbeat. But we couldn't learn anything else. All we could do was wait. The nurse said we should come in for another ultrasound in two weeks. It felt like we had entered a new type of pregnancy, one I hadn't expected to be in. *Would both twins survive? Would one of them? Would one or both of them be healthy? If the smaller embryo survived, but had a genetic abnormality, then what? Would we consider aborting one of them, or both?*

Michelle and I returned to the car, and took a moment to talk about the appointment. Mostly, we just sat there, remaining quiet in the shadowed garage parking lot. I felt cold. I didn't yet have words to describe how I was feeling emotionally, nor did Michelle. I put the car in drive, and we picked up Finnley from daycare.

After we arrived home, fed Finnley dinner, and put him to bed, Michelle and I sat on the couch. We did a lot of that after the appointment – sitting. It matched our energy levels.

I looked at her. She looked at me.

I wanted to talk about all the possibilities, all of the what ifs, but Michelle didn't want to hear them. She said, "I understand where you're coming from, but I can't be that person for you."

I was a planner. A doer. A person who solves problems. But Michelle simply needed time to sit and process. I sat quietly with my disappointment. Michelle felt that if she let the what ifs in, she would feel too much disappointment and sadness. We would know more about the embryos in two weeks, then go from there.

"Why don't you call one of your friends," she suggested. It was a good idea, but I didn't pick up the phone until several weeks later.

A few days before the second ultrasound appointment, I found myself in a bank parking lot. I sat in the car, having just deposited some money at the walk-up ATM. My eyes caught sight of a mama duck and her two ducklings trailing behind her. Their home had been bisected by concrete and several busy lanes of traffic. On each end of the parking lot, there was a wet riparian area – full of tall trees and dense vegetation. The ducks began to cross the street, attempting to go from one section of stream to another. I sat paralyzed as the mama duck led her two waddling babies in between the steady flow of rush-hour traffic. A few cars slowed. Some swerved.

I had seen this duck before – a few weeks earlier.

Only then, she had been leading five ducklings instead of only two.

The mama duck was determined to cross the street as cars entered and exited the busy highway ramps. A woman stopped her car in the middle of the road and began to chase the ducks, attempting to shoo them up a hillside. The woman's arms flapped, but the bird did not take flight. The mama duck kept walking forward. Another woman in a different car also attempted to chase the ducks. The chaos caused one of the ducklings to be separated from its mother and sibling. Mama duck began to panic, and her tiny webbed feet hit the pavement even harder. I thought they might all get hit by the oncoming cars, unaware of the situation ahead. I held my breath.

By this time I had exited the bank parking lot. I drove only a small distance, then sat parked at the intersection. I turned on my flashers. I could not leave. Could not look away.

I felt moved by those two women who had attempted to help. My heart ached with sadness knowing that no matter how hard we try, sometimes it's not enough. Sometimes there are things we cannot control.

The tears I'd held onto for the last two weeks finally came. I saw the mama and her two remaining ducklings finally make it across the street. The three of them waddled their way into the small patch of urban forest. I thought about Michelle. I wondered if we would lose one of the embryos, or even both.

When at the next ultrasound it was confirmed, only one heartbeat instead of two, I was flooded by a mix of emotions. Sadness. Relief. Confusion. Anger. More sadness.

I hadn't heard stories of other mothers or parents experiencing the loss of a vanishing twin. I didn't know how common it was. I didn't know where to turn for support. I had experienced a loss, but what kind? What *exactly* had I lost? Would the remaining fetus continue to grow into a healthy baby? I did not have answers to these questions. But it felt like I was holding onto a secret, so tiny and so big, I didn't know what to do with it. How to share it, or if I should.

I thought about all the prospective parents who had experienced loss before me. Loss in the form of negative pregnancy tests, miscarriages, failed IVF attempts, and bad news from adoption agencies. The line between life and loss is not always clean. It can be messy. And blurred. And complicated.

No matter what happened, I still had my son. Some people spend years trying to bring a child into their lives, but never turn their hopes into reality. I already had a child. I could give thanks for all the moments I had already experienced.

I had been there from the beginning. From conception, to birth, to adoption. I had held a small baby in my arms. Smelled my son's newness. Felt his warmth. No matter what happened, I would be his mother forever and always. I would be there when he needed help crossing the street. Be there until he was ready to let go of my hand, and walk on his own.

I thought of our one remaining *peanut* growing bigger and healthier with each passing day. I tried to remain hopeful. I tried to imagine how our lives would change with two children instead of one. I hoped that Finnley would get to share his life with a sibling. There were no guarantees, but he would probably get to meet his new baby sister or brother later that year.

24

DONOR SIBLINGS

When Michelle and I chose the sperm bank we used, we assumed that there would be other people who had also used the same sperm we did. But when we signed the multipage contract after purchasing those first few IUI vials, we had assumed that the sperm bank was setting strict limits on how many other families there would be. Mostly, my thoughts were preoccupied by how we were going to start *our* family, not someone else's.

When Michelle became pregnant with our second child, I started to think about other children who had resulted from the same sperm. A friend from our Queer Group had mentioned that she had connected in-person with a mother who had used the same sperm she had. Our friend told us there was an online portal which she used to connect with the mom. *Wow. Maybe we could do this too.* I thought. But did we want to? Maybe there were other kids who shared some of the same genetics as Finnley and the baby growing inside of Michelle. I was hesitant about the idea at first. I knew that once I learned information about the other families, I wouldn't be able to *unlearn* it. Would the information affect how I viewed myself? Would it affect how I thought about Finnley? Would it make me feel more insecure about my lack of genetic connection with my children?

I called the sperm bank and asked about the online portal. Sure enough, there was one. Only families with recorded live births using a particular donor could view each other's information. We were assigned a sibling number, S-10. Michelle and I discussed how we both felt. We each still had reservations, but we started to feel some curiosity and excitement. We decided to do an initial scan of the information.

When we logged into the portal, we could see that other families had registered with other numbers, such as S-3, S-4, S-5, etc. I could only assume that the numbers were being given out sequentially. The more live births there were, the more numbers there would be. There were indeed other families who had used *Mr. Handsome with a Side of Good Genetics* and they had real live kids!

The online portal was technologically basic. It was a single webpage, where various people could leave a message for everyone else to see. A few parents had posted about their child, listing approximate birth date or where they lived. Michelle and I quickly absorbed the information. When our eyes landed on a picture of a boy with bright red hair, who looked remarkably like Finnley, my mind was blown! Finnley had a doppelgänger who was related to him and lived in Europe! *That*, I had not expected.

My mind went back to the contract we signed. It mentioned the company's presence in other countries, but I assumed donor sperm stayed in the country of origin. That was not the case. The sperm bank had shipped sperm from our donor all over the world. At the time, there were donor conceived children who shared some of Finnley's genetics in the U.S. and in at least five other countries around the globe!

After reading the parent's comments and looking at the kids' pictures, we noticed a comment from a mom named Heather, who also lived on the West Coast. Heather mentioned that the group of parents had formed a separate group on a messaging app because it facilitated easier communication. Michelle messaged Heather and got us both added to the group. Parents from all over the world introduced themselves. Again, my mind was blown! Every single one of their kids was genetically related to Finnley.

Only two weeks after joining the group, Heather private messaged me and Michelle. She and her wife Tiffany were going to be visiting Seattle. They recognized it might feel too soon to meet in person, but still wanted to know if we were up for it. Their son Jack was only one year older than Finnley.

At first, it was unsettling to learn that there were at least ten other families who had used the same sperm as we did. I had expected some kids, but it seemed like a lot. It *felt* like a lot. Would we tell Finnley that he had brothers and sisters? When and how? Would Finnley be upset with me and Michelle for discovering there were so many?

Initially, I worried that this information would make him feel different or not normal. As an adult, I could see how creating those categories as a child no longer served me well. I had grown up in a household that was frequently tumultuous and where I felt unsafe. But I was providing such a different experience for my son. I was present. I was emotionally connected. I would always keep him safe. There was no doubt that being raised by two moms was going to influence Finnley's childhood, but maybe he could share his experience with all these other kids.

Michelle and I said yes to Heather's invitation. My curiosity had grown. Who were Heather and Tiffany? What were they like? Which one of them gave birth to Jack and why? Did the non-bio mother ever feel like me? Would Jack look at all like Finnley? Would the children share any behavioral traits?

After Heather and Tiffany arrived in Seattle, they reached out and we planned to meet at a park. Michelle and I got there a little early and Finnley went straight to the playground. I saw a red Prius, park nearby on the street. Two women with short hair and a young child got out of the car. I immediately tagged this family as our crew. When they walked across the street and introduced themselves, I had been right.

The August day was sunny and hot. Our two sweaty kids ran around the playground chasing one another. Finnley still wasn't great at running yet given his girthy legs, but he tried to keep up with Jack. When the two kids got close to one another, Finnley hit Jack on the head. Their bond didn't seem instantaneous or magical. They acted like two young children who had just met.

Michelle and I took turns watching the kids, while the other talked to Heather or Tiffany. They both seemed genuine in wanting to connect to us and described sincere engagement with the other donor sibling families. They asked some basic questions like where we worked, how long we had been in the area, and where we grew up. Then, the conversation turned more intimate.

Heather asked if we were planning on having a second child. Michelle and I looked at one another. We had briefly discussed if this question might come up beforehand. We agreed to tell them if it felt right.

Michelle said, "I'm sixteen weeks pregnant right now." The four of us smiled. They said they wanted to have at least one more kid in the future too. Tiffany had given birth to Jack and Heather wanted to get pregnant next. She seemed confident of her decision. I didn't know if she shared some of the insecurities I had felt with Finnley, but I could tell we did share something – a deep love for our kids. We also shared an interest in connecting other queer parents to one another. I had recently started my Second Parent project online.

As time went on and Michelle's belly again, began to grow, I continued to read the messages from the group. I went through ebbs and flows of wanting to stay connected. Sometimes the number of messages felt overwhelming. Ten families was already a lot – just how many more could there be? A few other families also said they had gotten pregnant again with their second child, so our pod continued to grow.

After only a few months, when one of the moms called the kids "siblings," I felt defensive. *My kid and your kid are not in the same family*, I thought. They're not *siblings*. My feelings came from wanting to protect what I had. Protect what I had fought so hard to create.

But with more time, I found myself wanting to genuinely understand more about the parents. I wanted to see pictures of their growing kids. I began to view the parents as individuals who were creative, humorous, and nurturing. There were lesbian moms and self-identified Single Mothers by Choice (SMC), a term I had never heard of before. I thought about these women carving out space for their own narratives, just like I had on my journey to becoming a non-biological parent. These women seemed confident in their choices. They seemed like badasses who I wanted to meet.

Maybe these genetically related kids and their parents could be a part our family too. Maybe we could be a part of theirs. I imagined that Finnley (and our second kid) would likely only feel connected to a small handful of these children. But maybe he would feel deeply connected to others. By staying in the group, I was keeping a door open in the future. And in the meantime, Michelle and I could get to know the parents better. I didn't have a genetic connection with any of these people, but it didn't matter. It mattered that I surrounded my kids around loving, caring, and supportive people – which these families seemed to be.

After a few more months of communicating with the other mothers, I eventually felt comfortable with the term "half-sibling," to describe how the kids were connected. When I said it out loud, it made sense to me. Our kids shared some genetic material, but there was also room for so much more. It left room for the biological parents. It left room for individual experiences. As a lesbian, non-bio mom, it also left room for me. I could envision myself fitting into the other "half," even if the math didn't quite add up.

When Heather and Tiffany visited again, it was to meet our second child who had recently turned one. Our two families met at a pizza shop in north Seattle. Jack and Finnley ran around the kids' play area making a mess, while us moms ate pizza and caught up. Our newly walking daughter, toddled around the table. I savored the moment. Here I was, a mom for the second time. And there were three kids in the room who all shared a genetic connection, but came from two different families. It felt incredible.

When I asked if Heather was still planning on getting pregnant, she said she was currently a few months along. Michelle and I both gave our congratulations. We would soon be welcoming yet another half-sibling into our group. I didn't know how many kids there would ultimately be, but the thought of having over fifty half-siblings all around the world, still left me feeling uneasy. But there wasn't anything to do. No planning. No organizing. No controlling. We had all made our decisions with the best information possible at the time. We simply had to enjoy our families as they were.

I had started my journey into parenthood when there were so many unknowns. With time, my previous definitions of the word *family* had cracked and rifted. It left space for new meanings – and new feelings too.

All the kids ran back to the table to eat more pizza. I imagined visiting Heather and Tiffany to meet their second child after they were born. I imagined going on family vacations to meet the other half-siblings around the world. I imagined the questions and conversations that would follow. As I hugged my two children sitting next to me, I felt stronger and more confident in my role than ever before. I was an adult. I was a mother. My journey into parenthood was just beginning.

ACKNOWLEDGEMENTS

I'd first like to the thank my friends who I entrusted the initial pages of my manuscript to – Erin and Kelly. You provided valuable feedback without judgement and always added a humorous note. To the grounded women who have been my guides – Mary Anne and Amaris. You told me to "just keep writing." You have helped teach me that the past is the past and the present is full of possibilities. To Pamela Erens who provided developmental and line editing. Your comments and questions made me dig deeper. Thank you to the queer parents who shared your stories of struggle, pride, and joy with me – I am always humbled by your experiences.

And lastly, to my family. I wouldn't have this story without you. For my wife Michelle, who showed unwavering support of this project from the beginning. From our initial conversations to the last readings of the manuscript, you've helped me see my strengths as a writer and a mother. And for that, I am forever grateful.

ABOUT THE AUTHOR

Lora Liegel lives in Bellingham, Washington with her wife and two children. From poetry to prose, she has been writing since her youth. This is her first book. Lora believes that every person has a story worth sharing. She started the Second Parent project to connect lesbian and queer, non-bio mothers with one another. These stories can be found online at second-parent.com or on Instagram @secondparent. When she is not writing or with her family, Lora can be found under the canopy of a northwest forest or walking alongside the ocean.

Made in the USA
Middletown, DE
16 July 2021